Adult Coloring Book

40 PURRTASTIC CATS

Stress Relieving Coloring Pages For Adults By

www.ColoringCraze.com

Copyright © 2017 ColoringCraze

All rights reserved.

ISBN: 153346135X
ISBN-13: 978-1533461353
Edition: 4

FREE GIFT FOR YOU!

Coloring books enthusiast? Get **Free Bonus Kit** from the site below:

=> http://www.coloringcraze.com/bonus <=

WWW.COLORINGCRAZE.COM

Test Your Colors Here

Blend Colors Here

___ MIX ___ ___ MIX ___ ___ MIX ___

___ MIX ___ ___ MIX ___ ___ MIX ___

___ MIX ___ ___ MIX ___ ___ MIX ___

WWW.COLORINGCRAZE.COM

Test Your Colors Here

Blend Colors Here

MIX MIX MIX

MIX MIX MIX

MIX MIX MIX

WWW.COLORINGCRAZE.COM

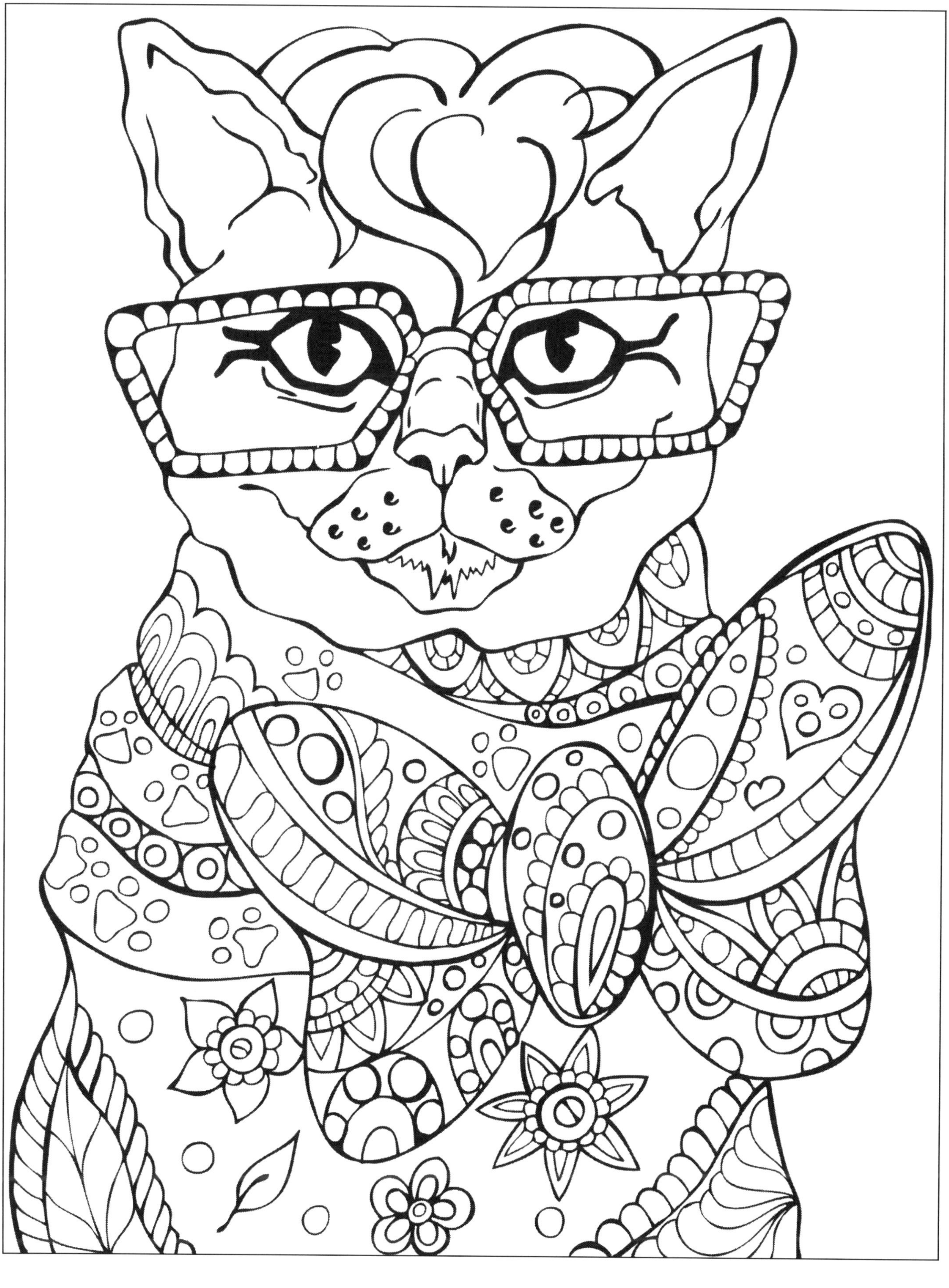

WWW.COLORINGCRAZE.COM

WWW.COLORINGCRAZE.COM

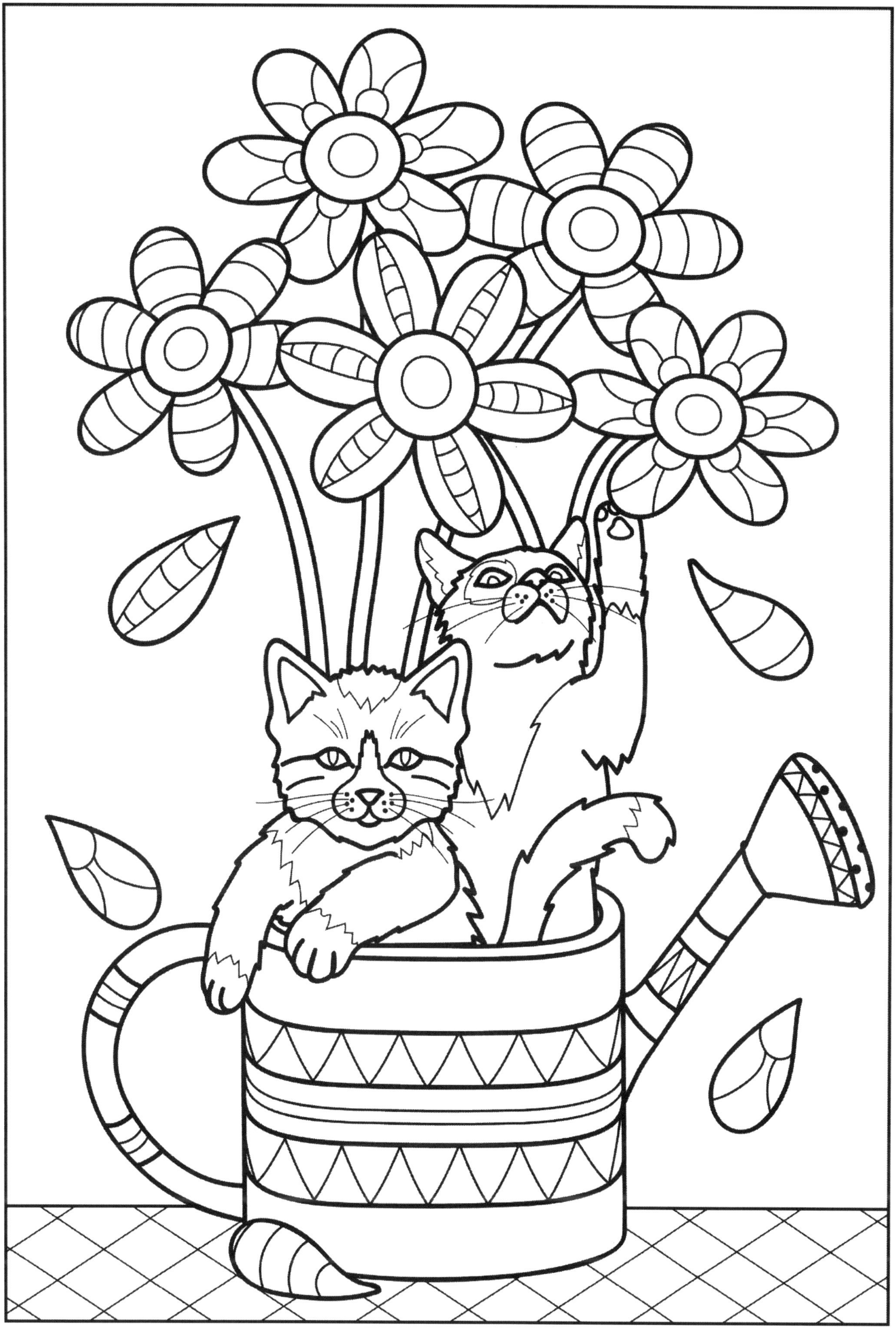

WWW.COLORINGCRAZE.COM

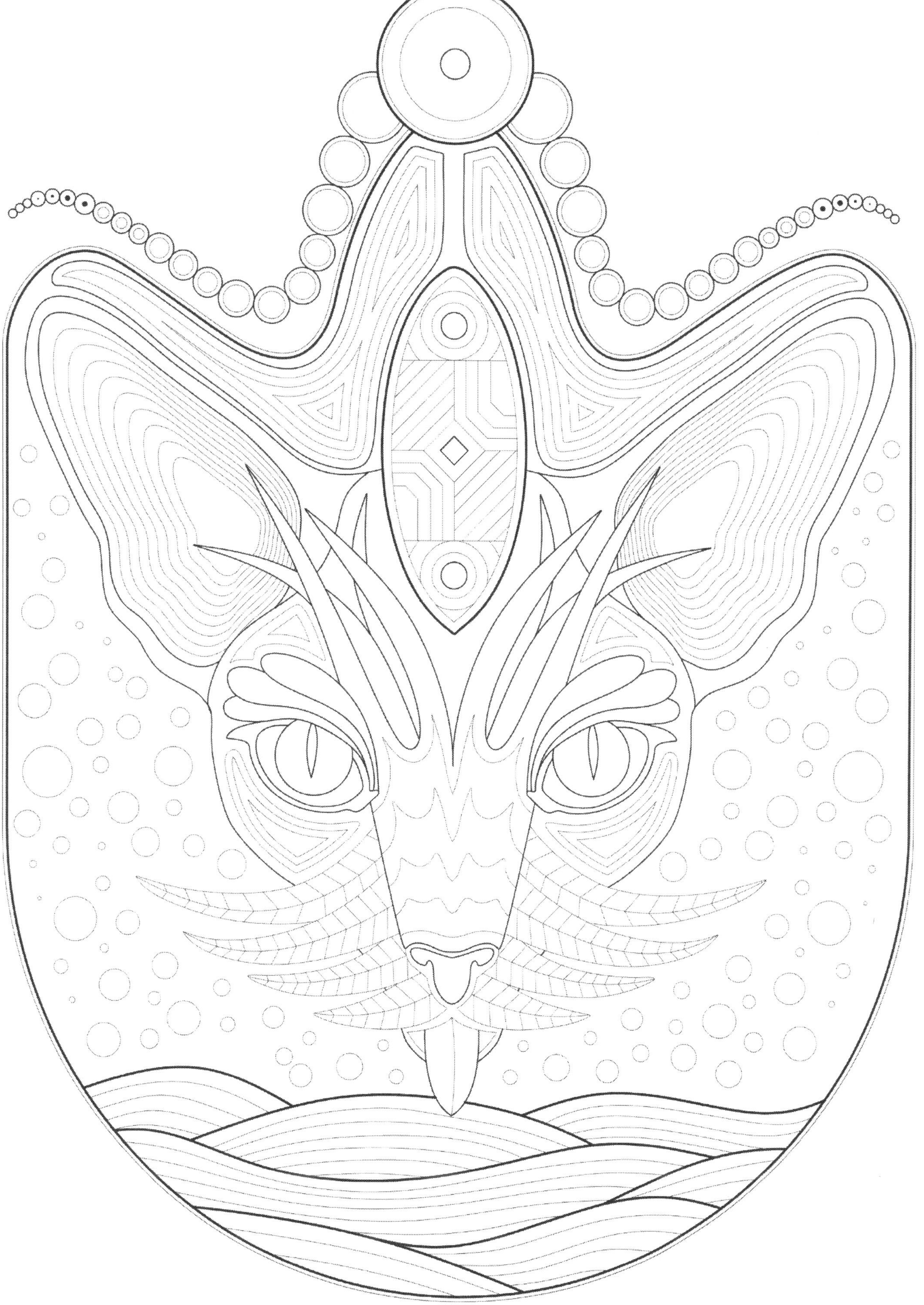

WWW.COLORINGCRAZE.COM

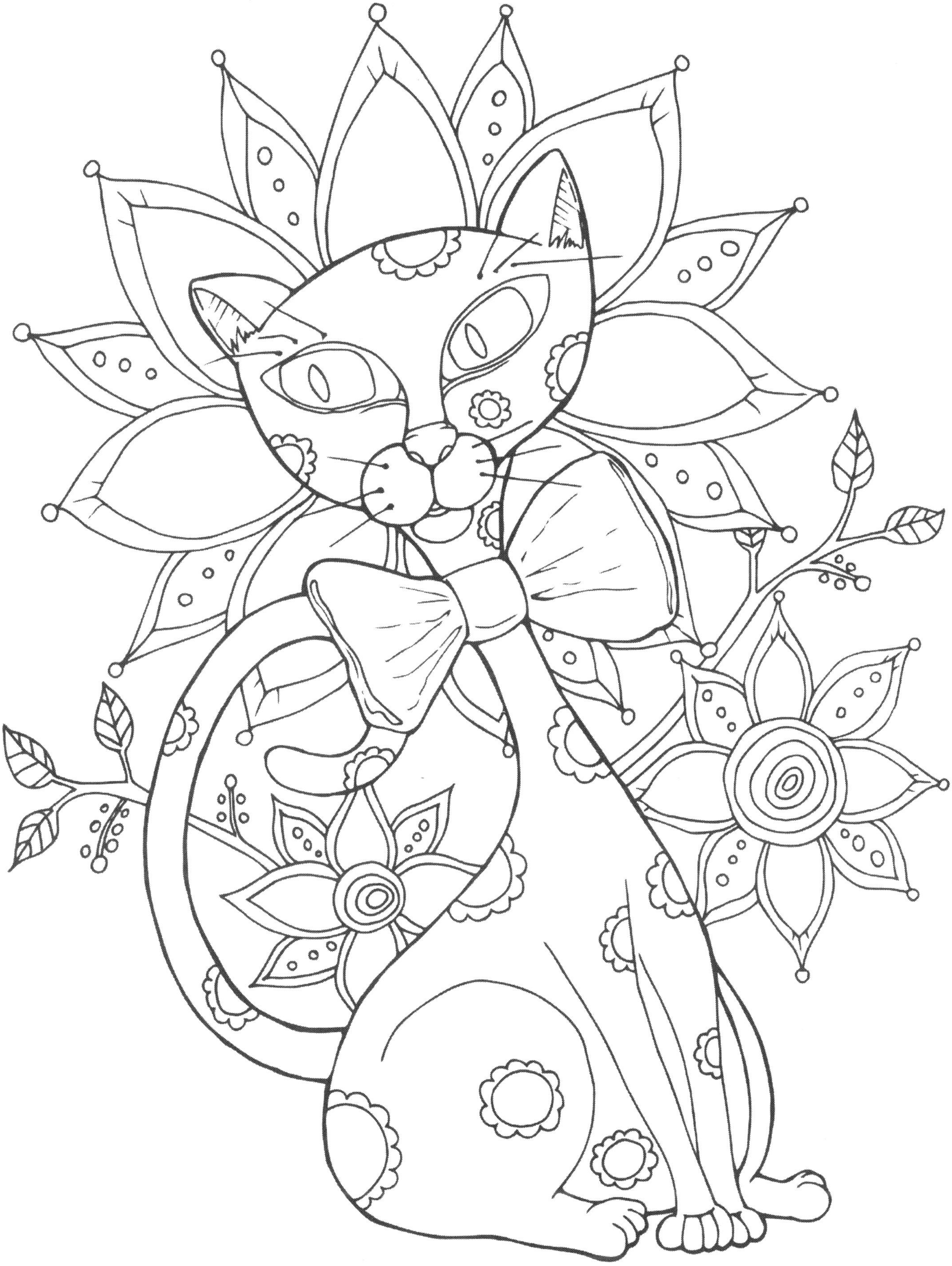

WWW.COLORINGCRAZE.COM

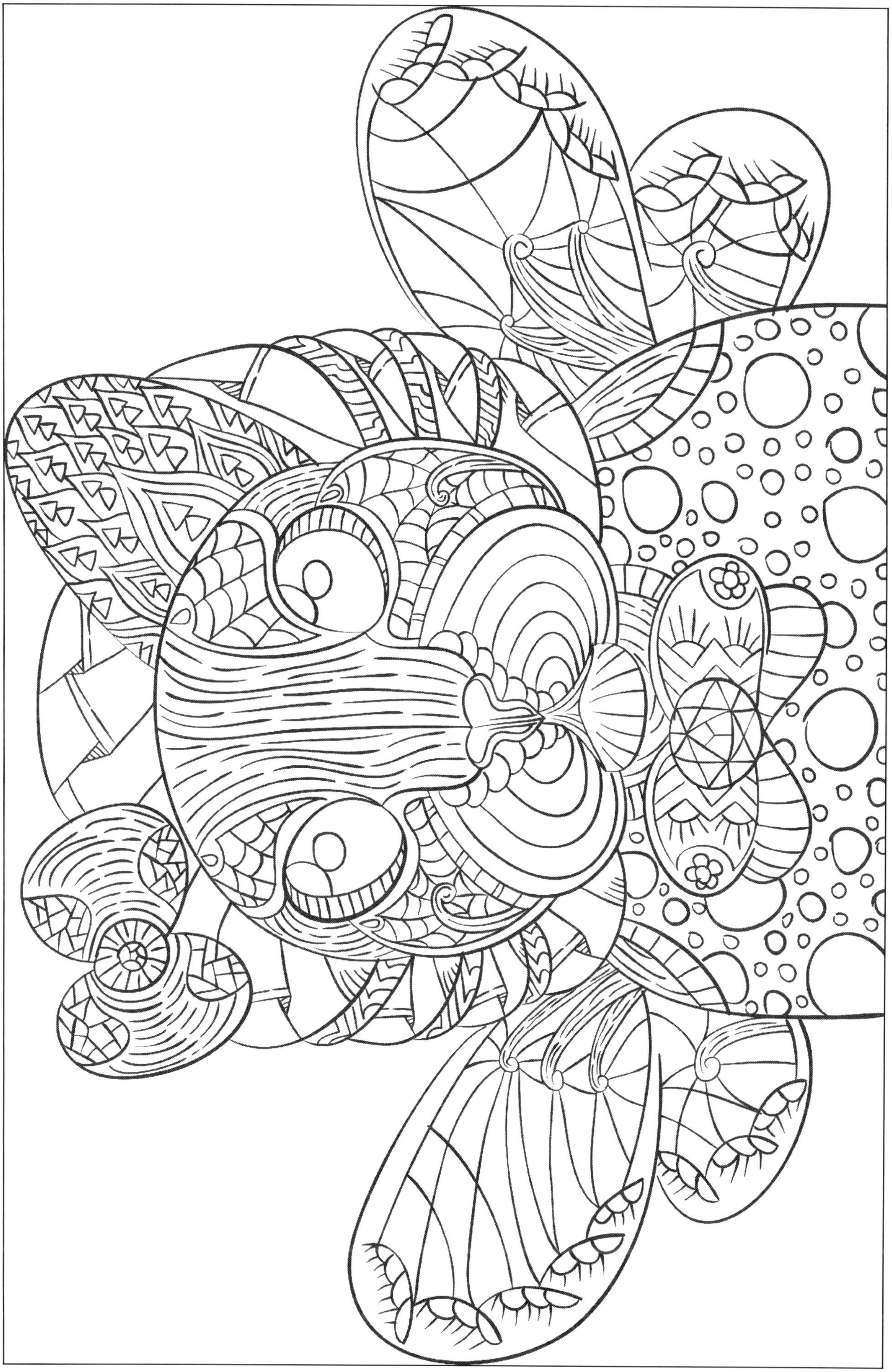

WWW.COLORINGCRAZE.COM

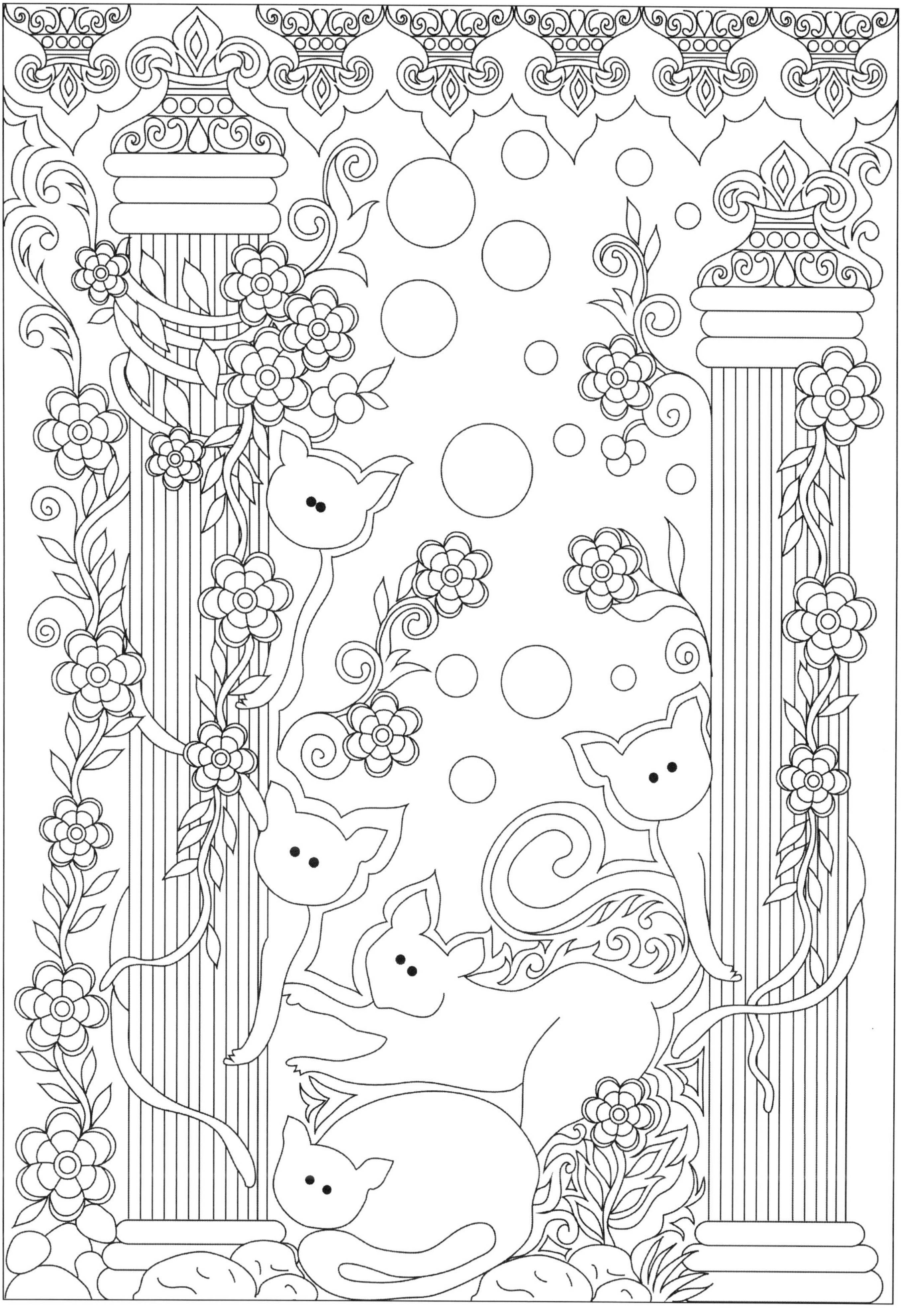

WWW.COLORINGCRAZE.COM

WWW.COLORINGCRAZE.COM

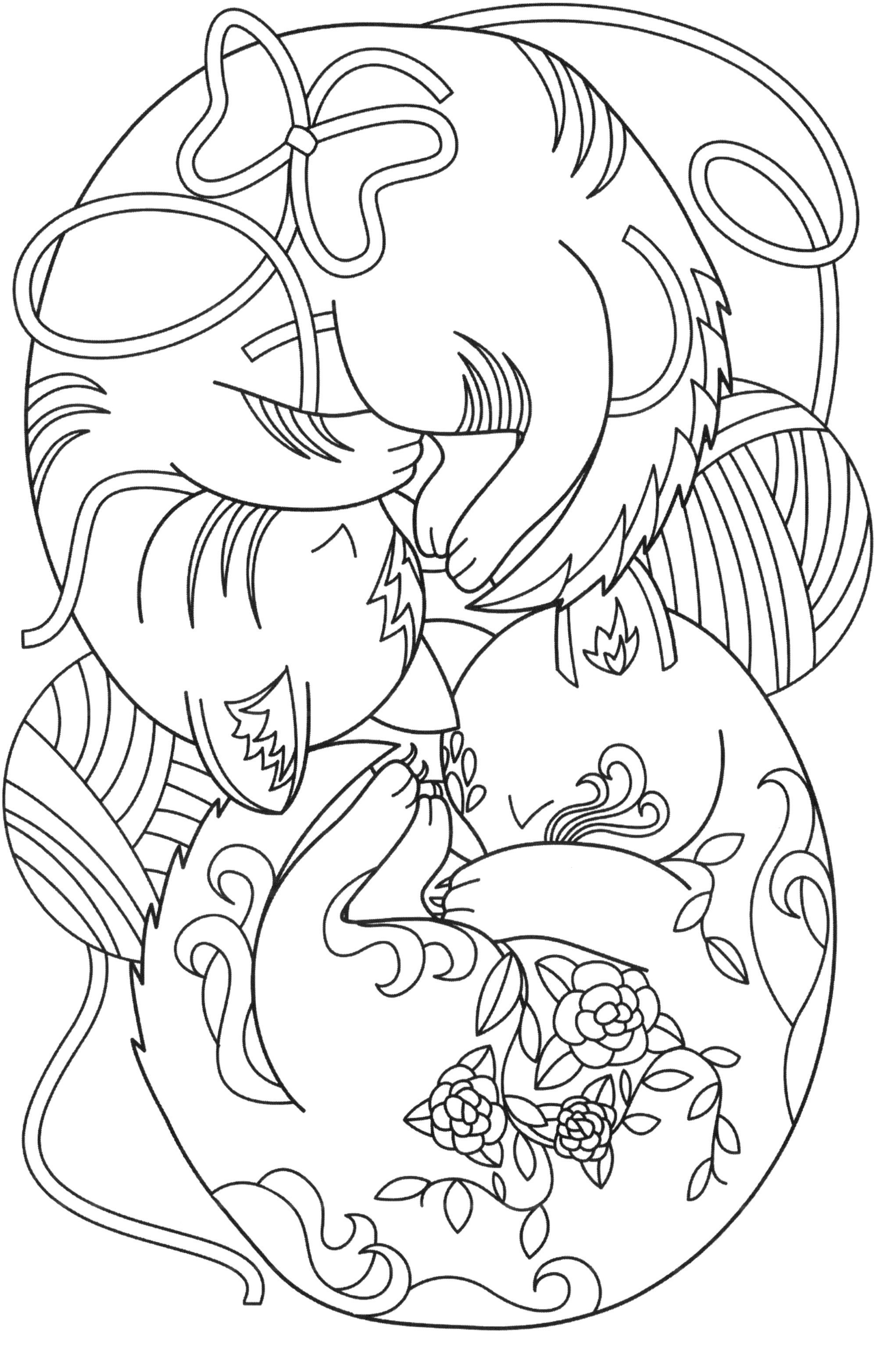

WWW.COLORINGCRAZE.COM

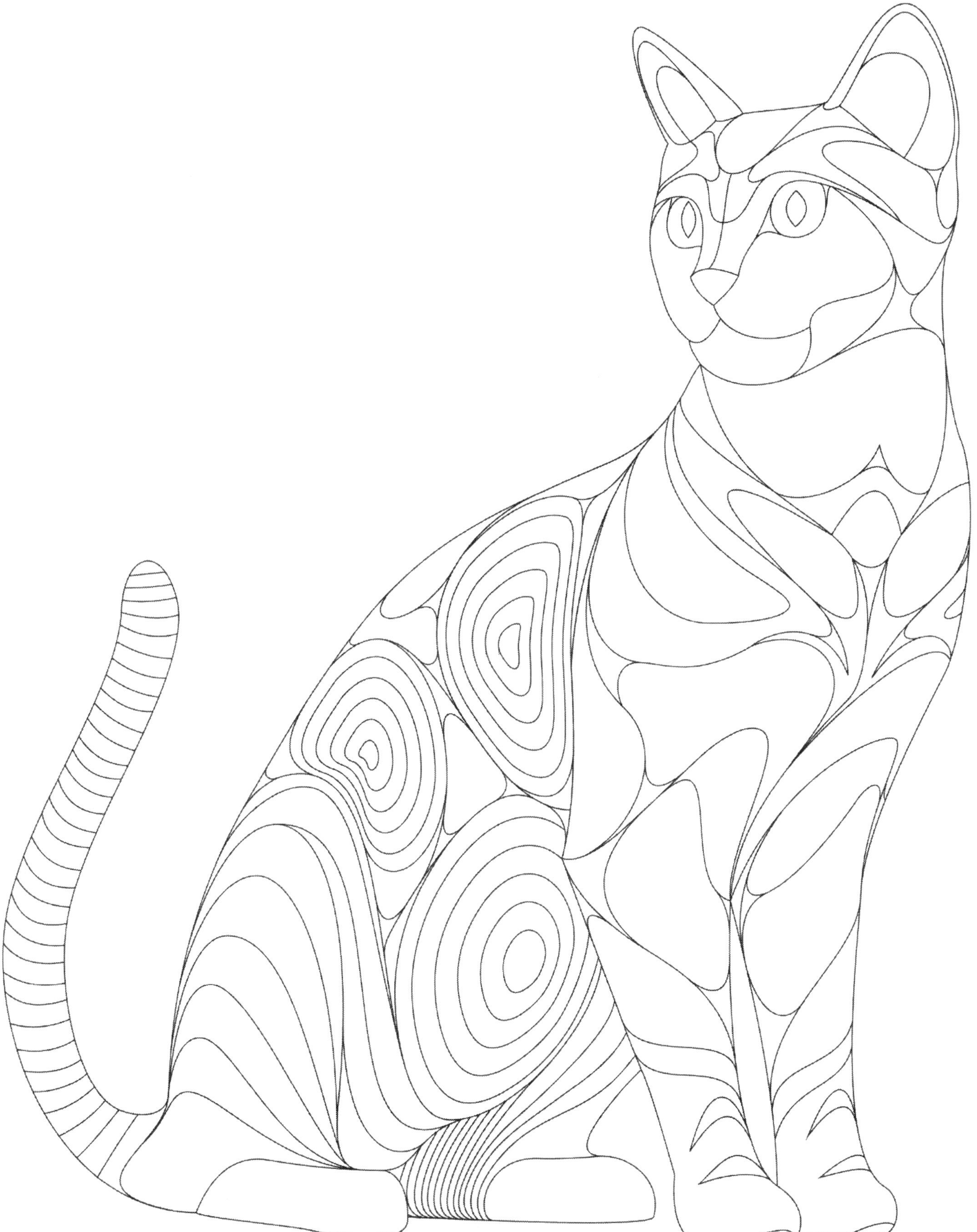

WWW.COLORINGCRAZE.COM

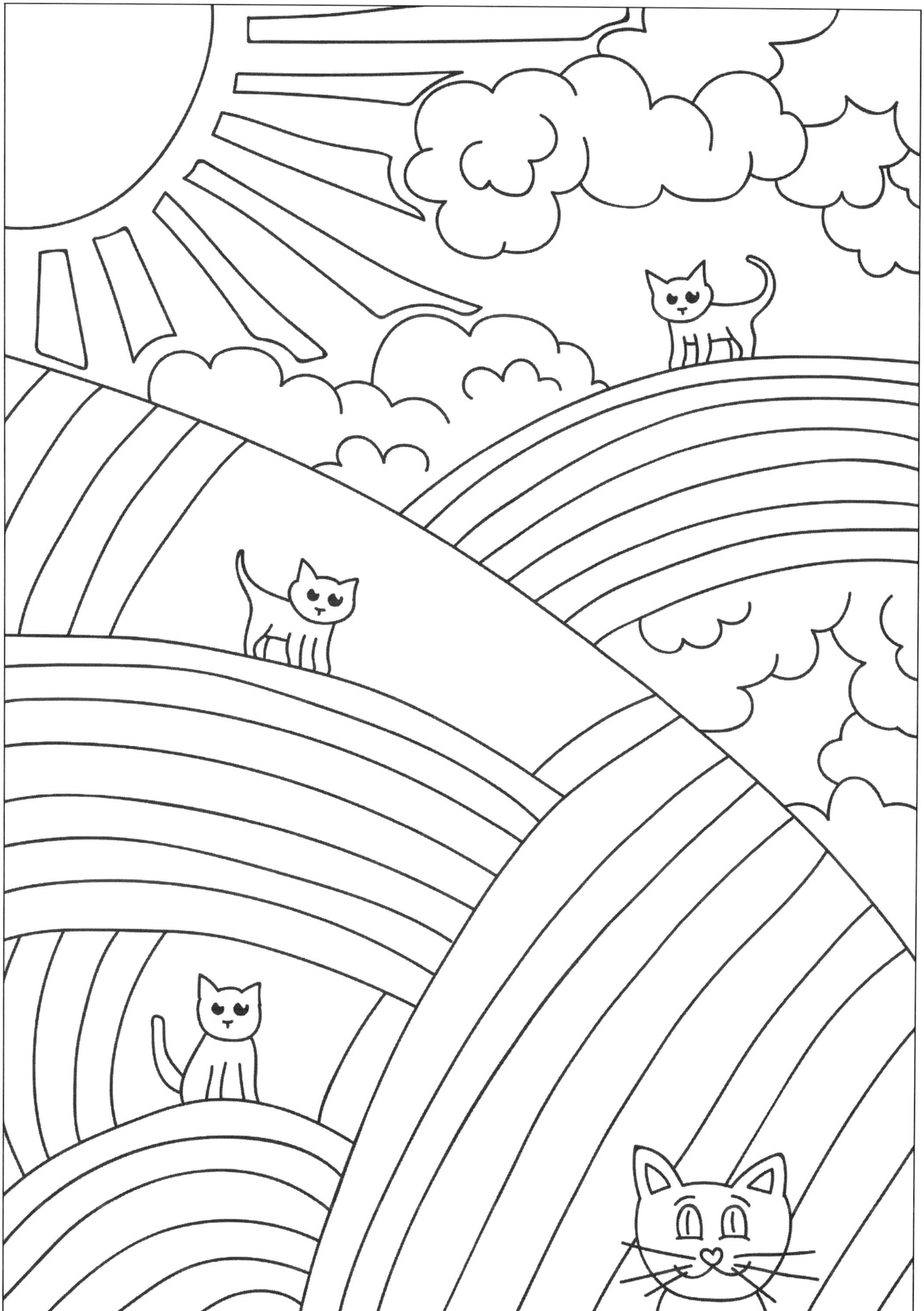

WWW.COLORINGCRAZE.COM

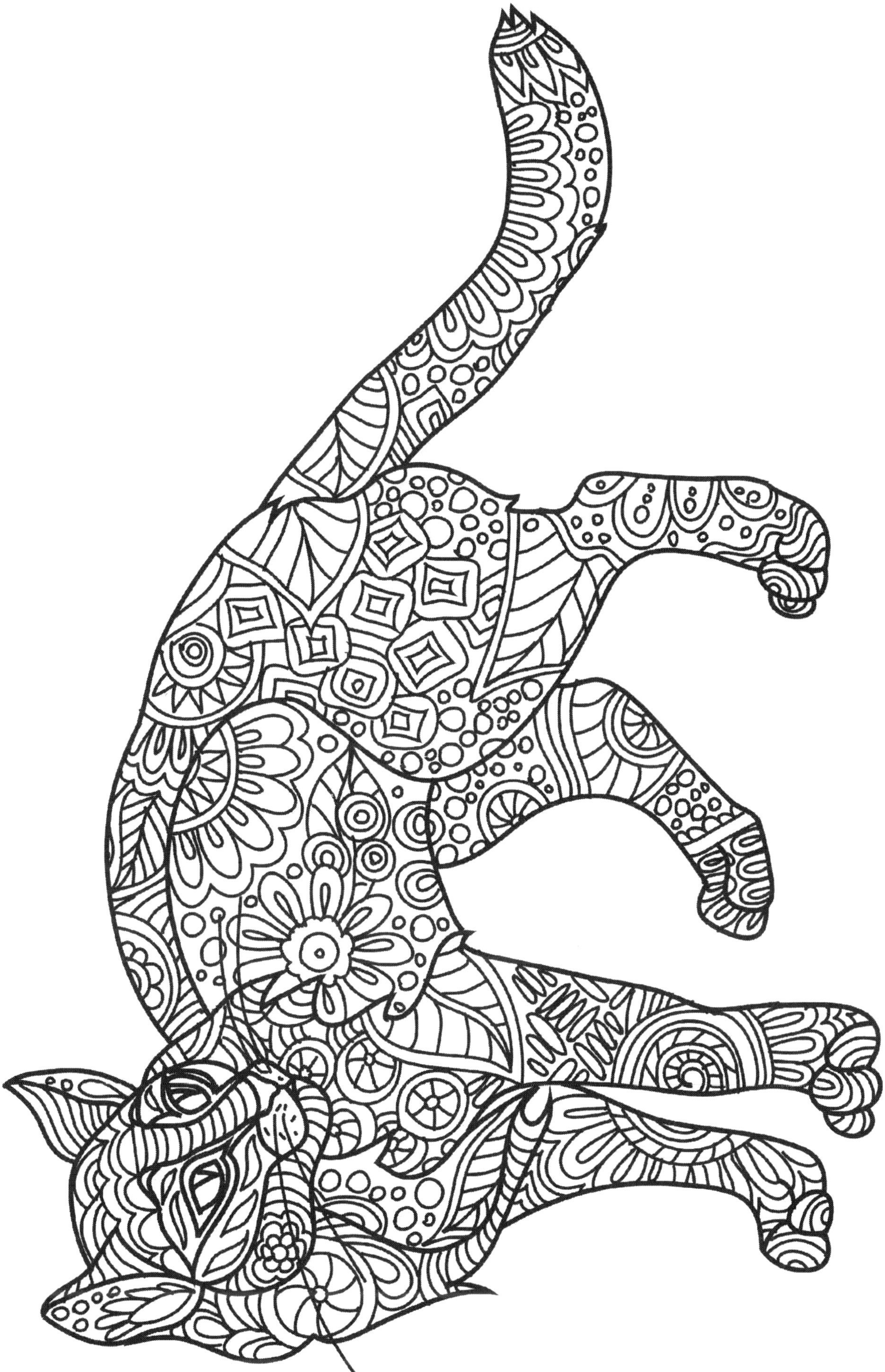

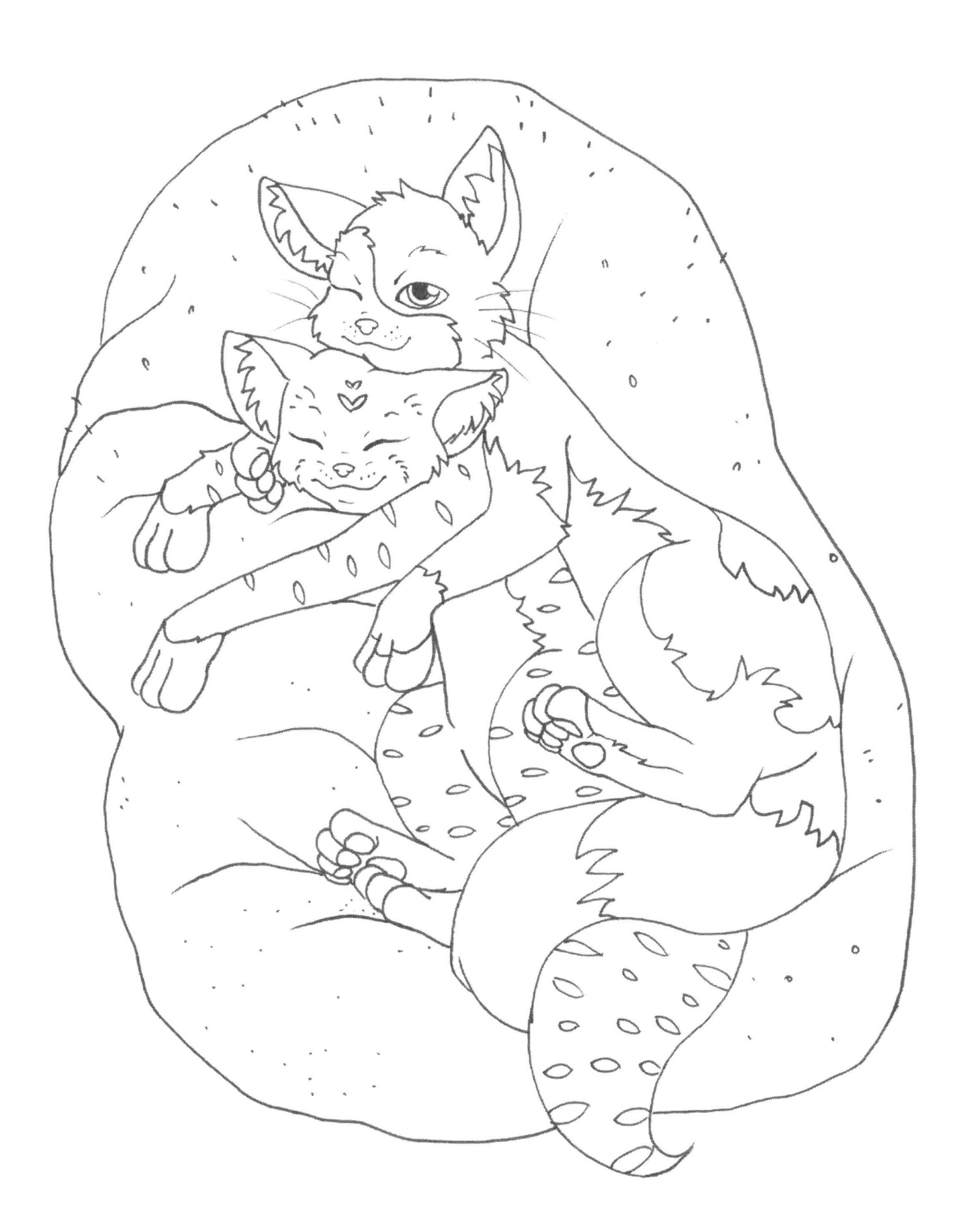

WWW.COLORINGCRAZE.COM

WWW.COLORINGCRAZE.COM

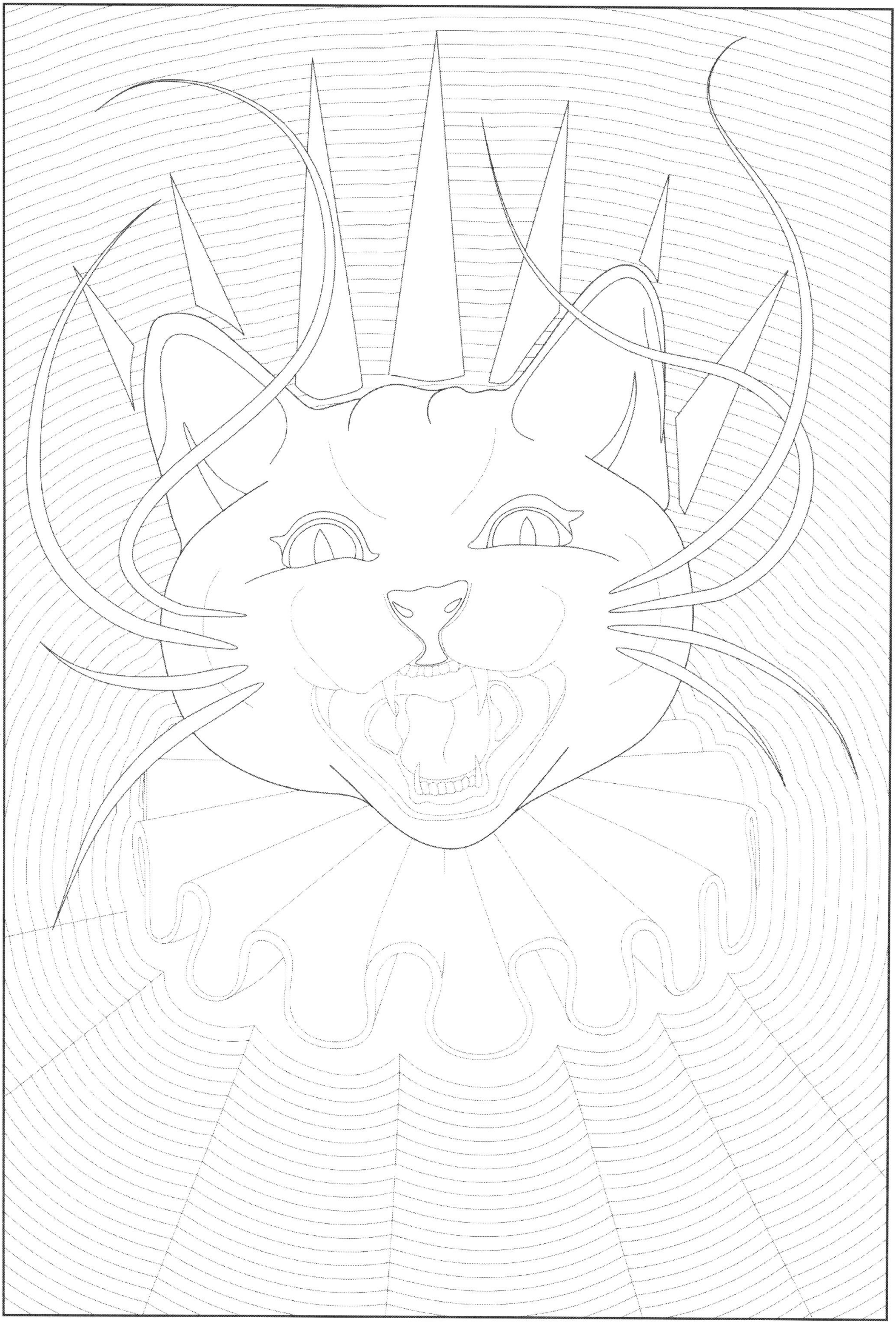

WWW.COLORINGCRAZE.COM

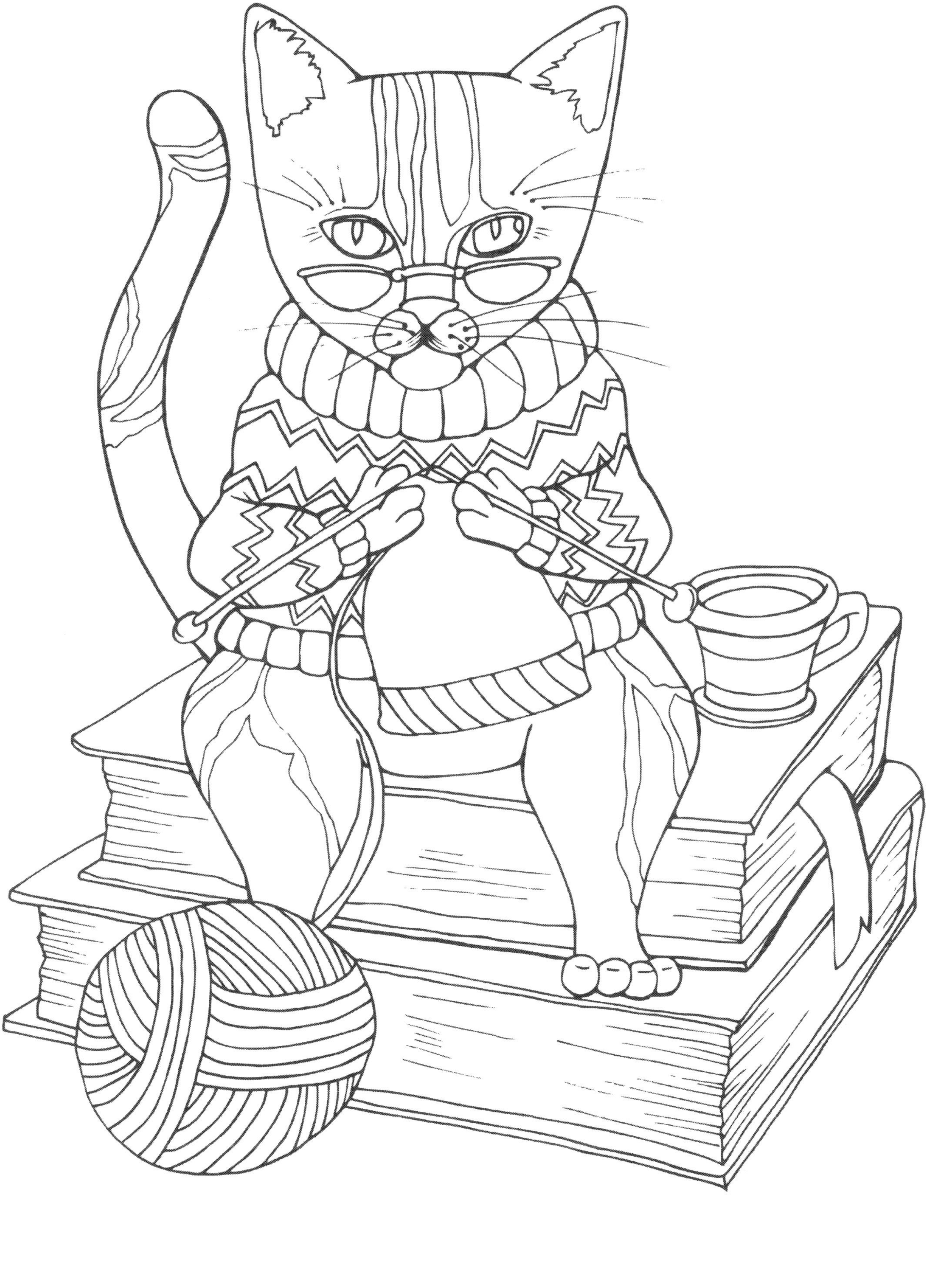

WWW.COLORINGCRAZE.COM

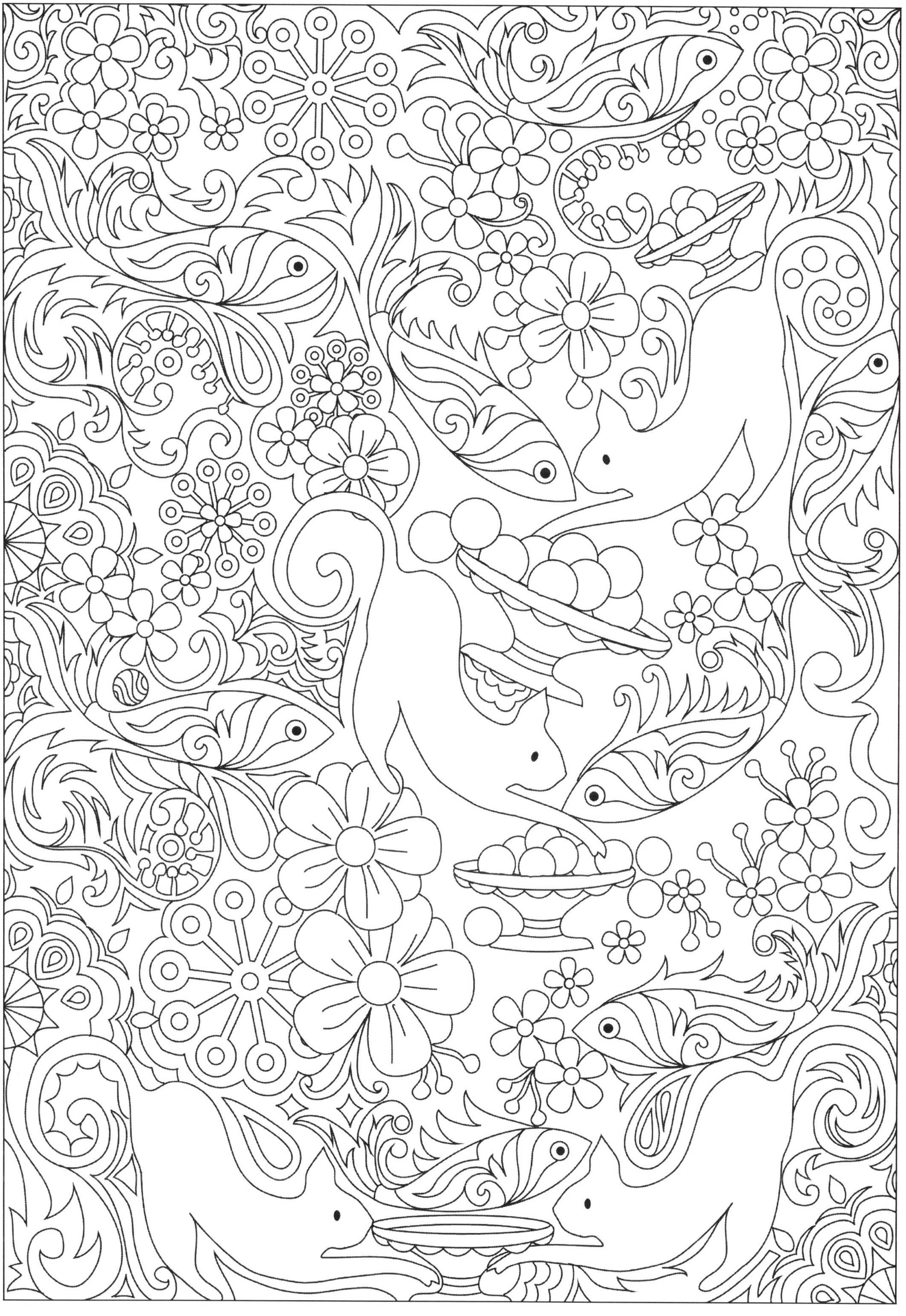

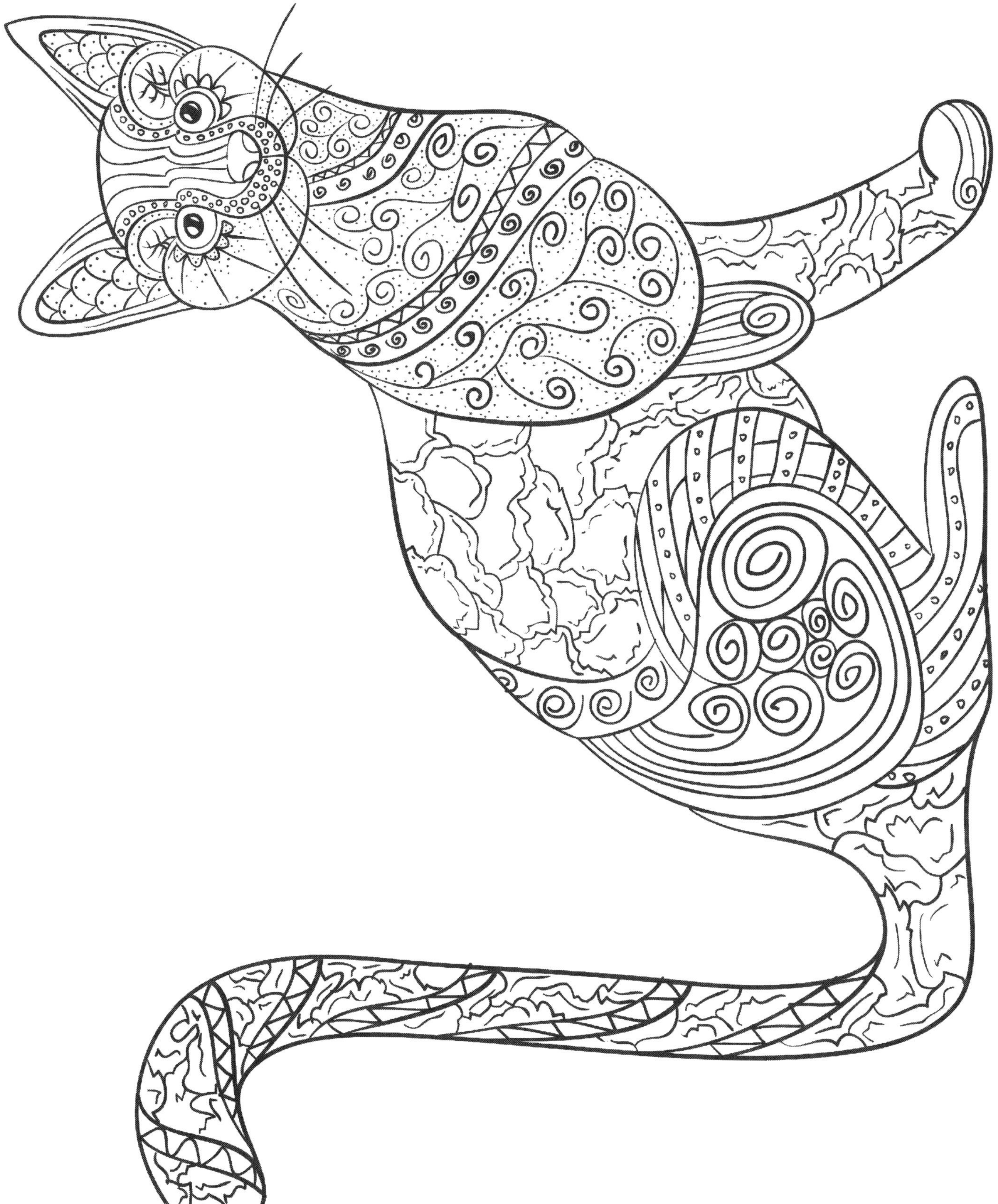

WWW.COLORINGCRAZE.COM

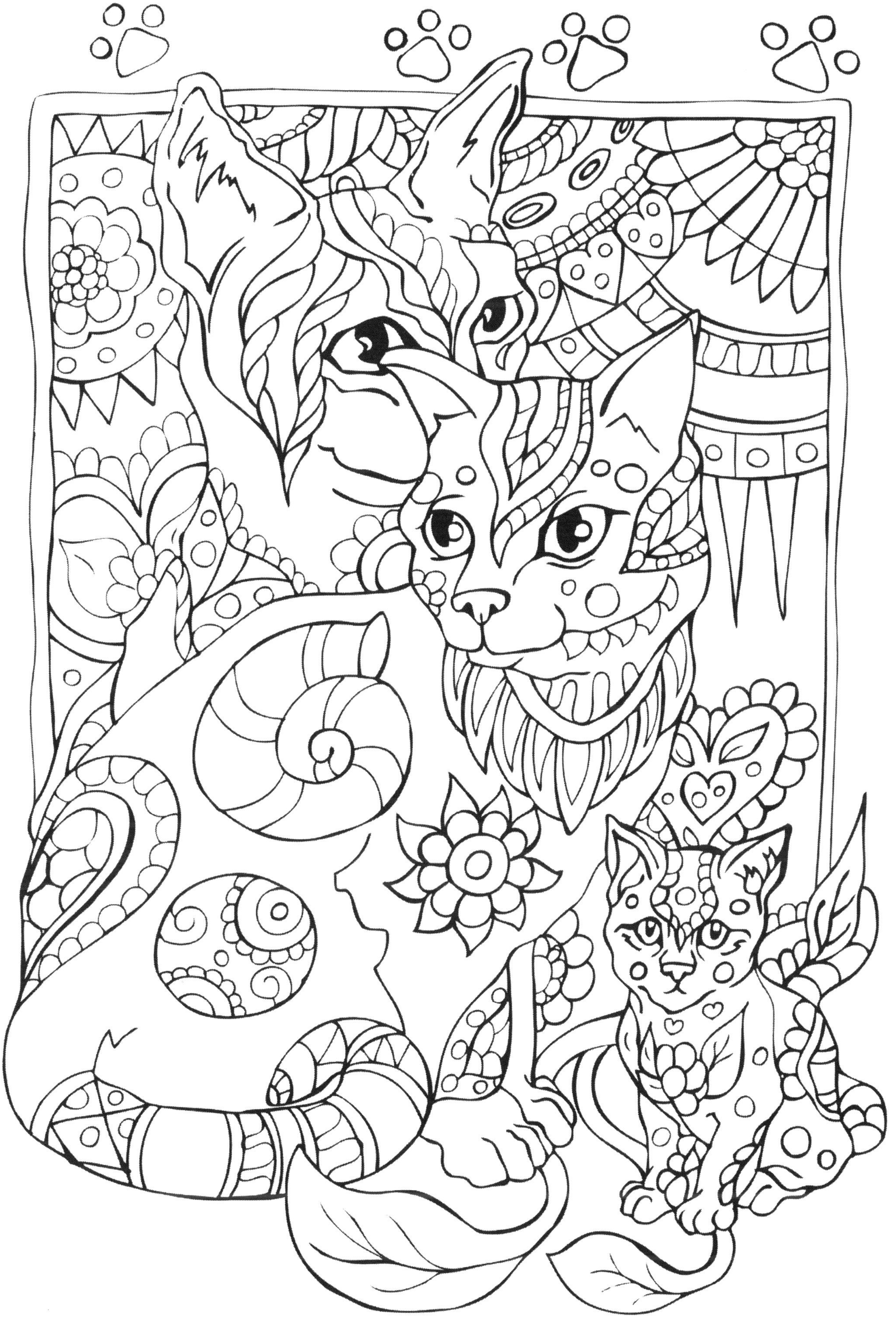

WWW.COLORINGCRAZE.COM

WWW.COLORINGCRAZE.COM

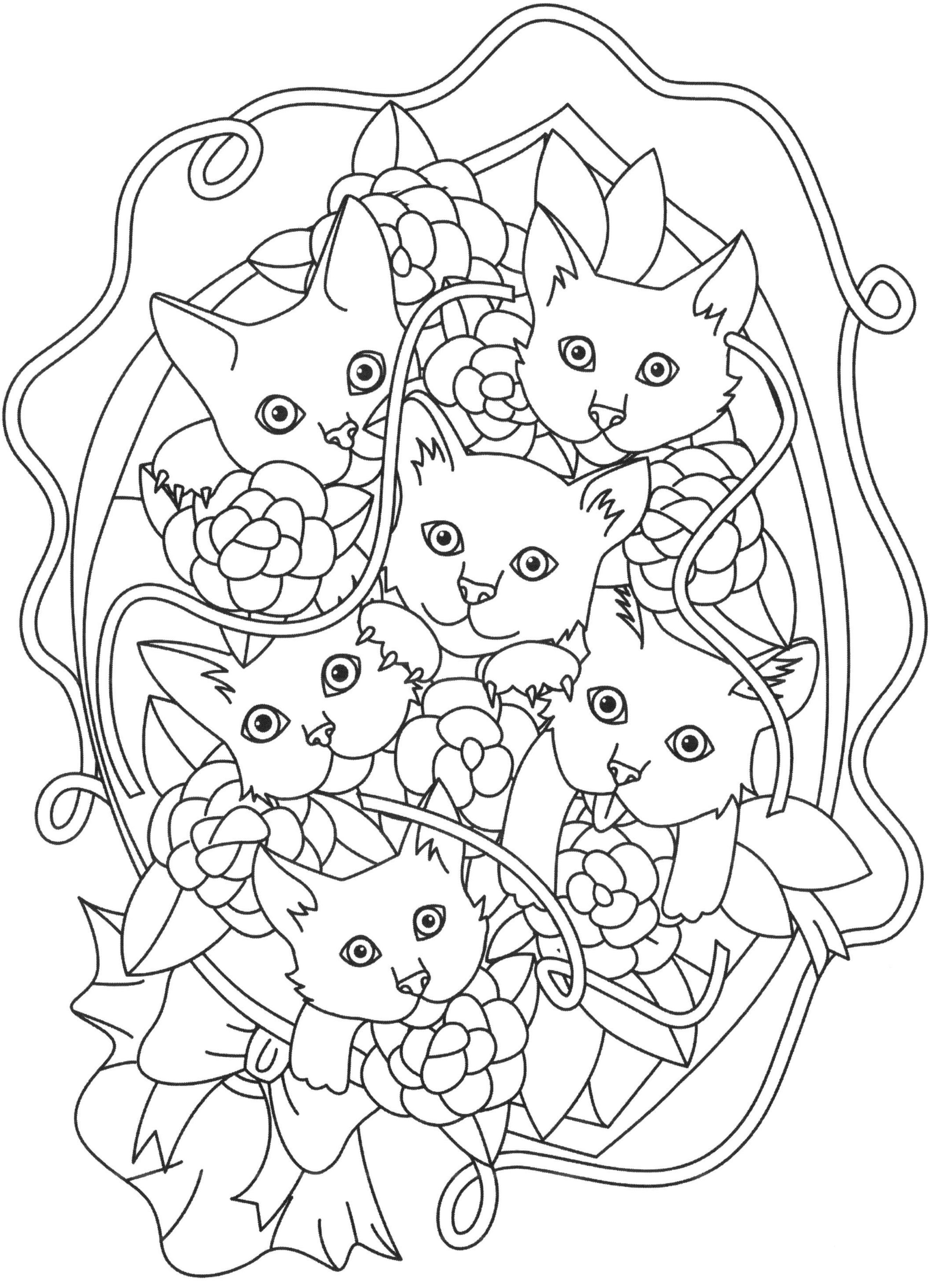

WWW.COLORINGCRAZE.COM

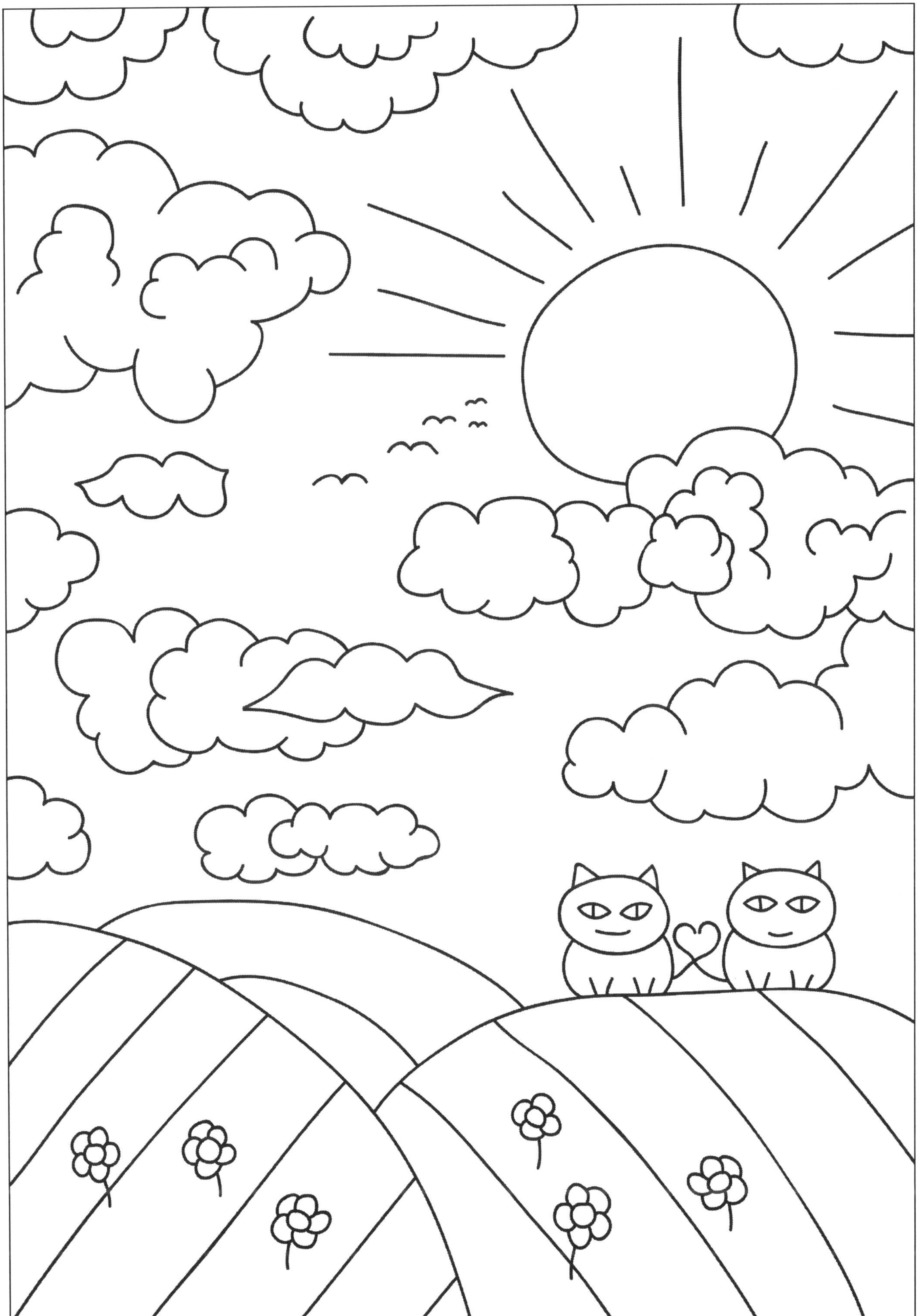

WWW.COLORINGCRAZE.COM

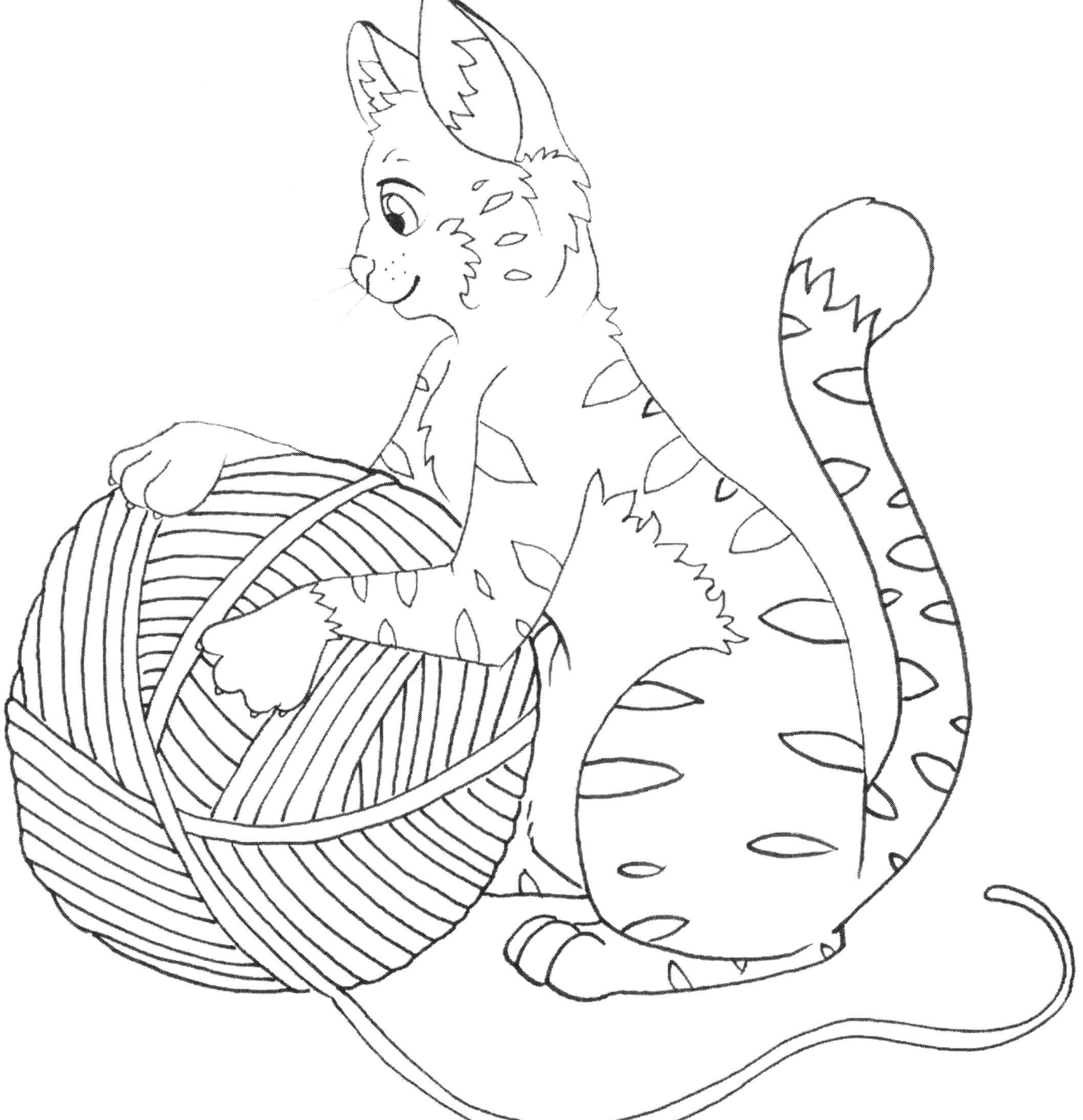

WWW.COLORINGCRAZE.COM

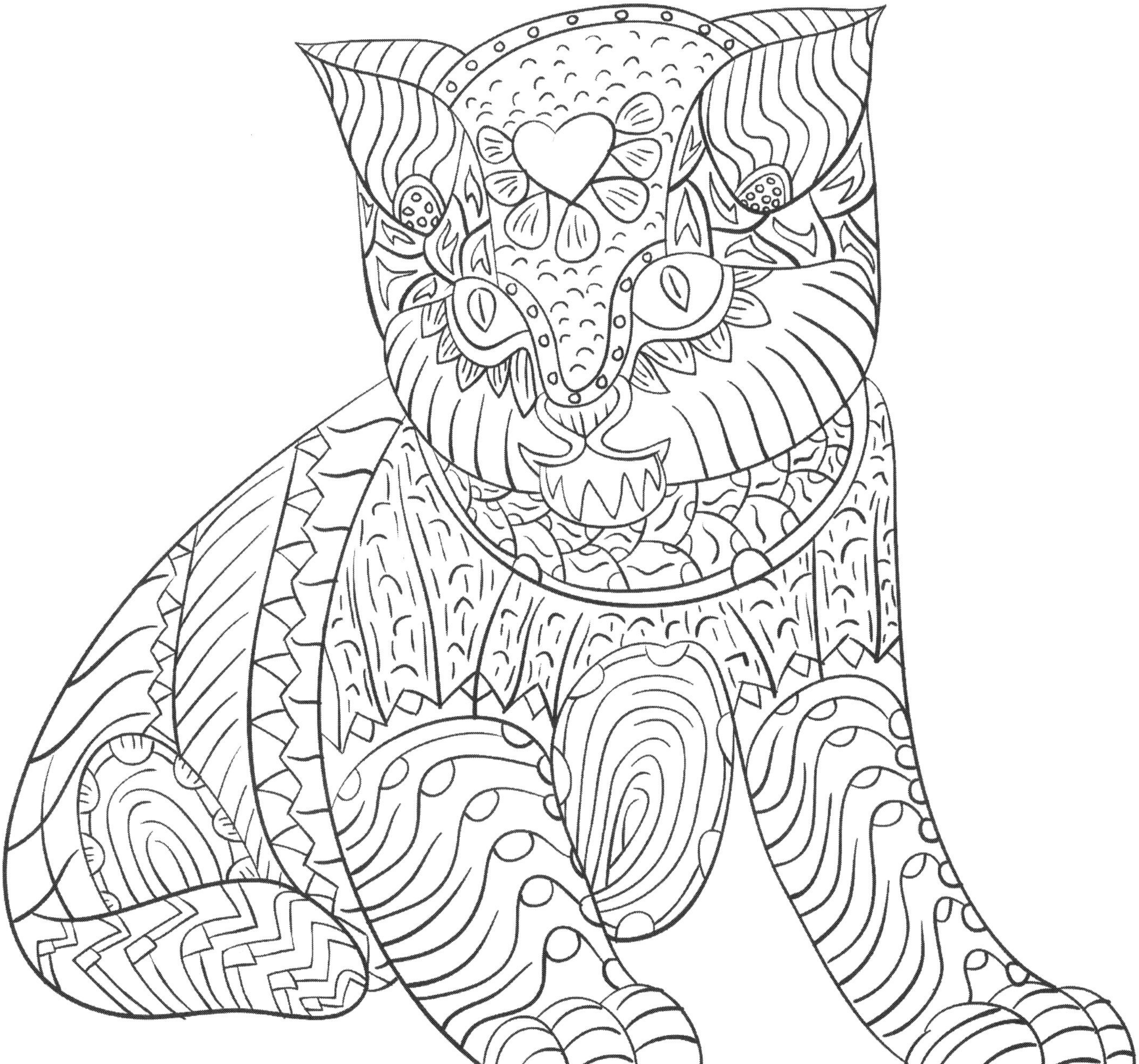

WWW.COLORINGCRAZE.COM

WWW.COLORINGCRAZE.COM

WWW.COLORINGCRAZE.COM

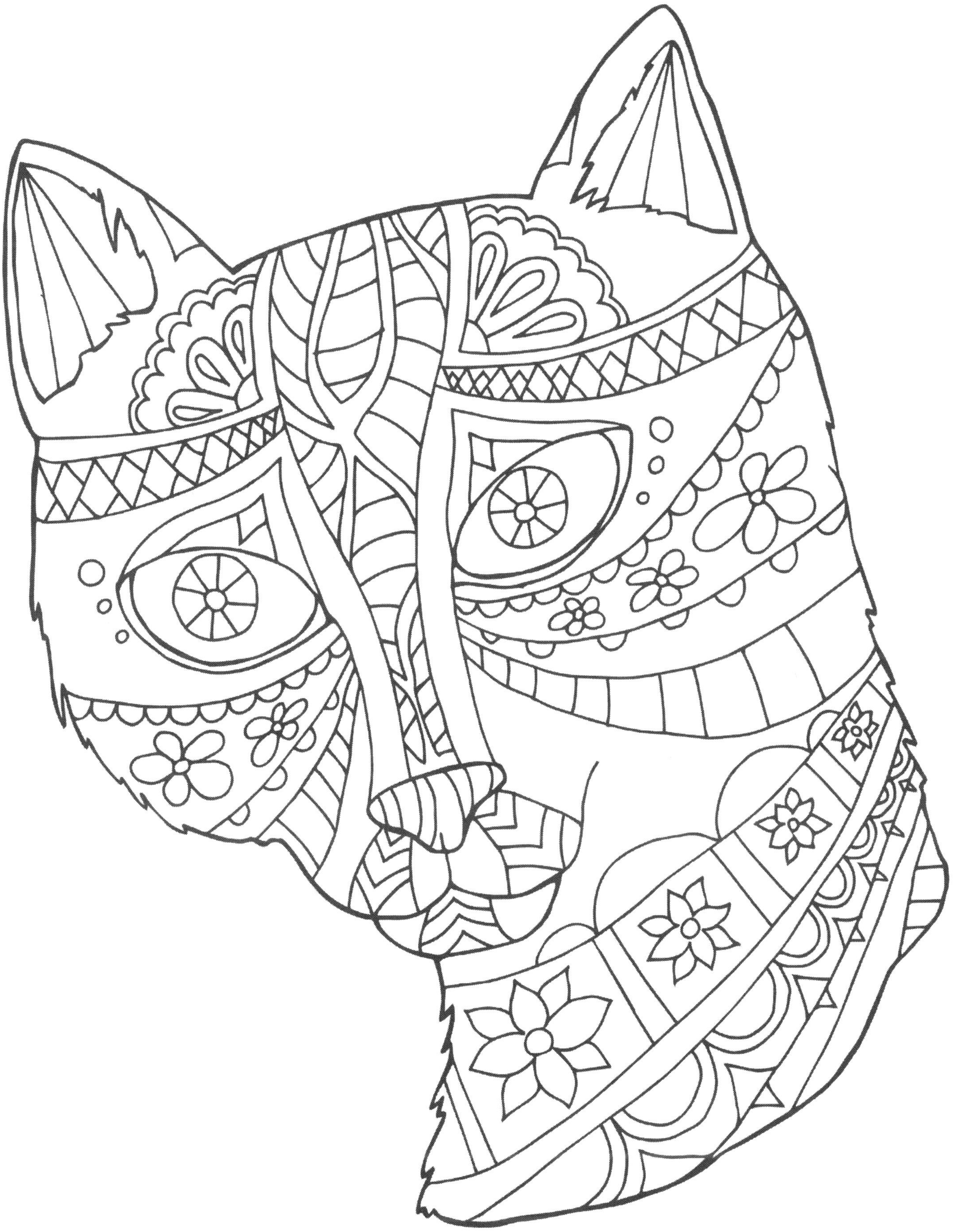

WWW.COLORINGCRAZE.COM

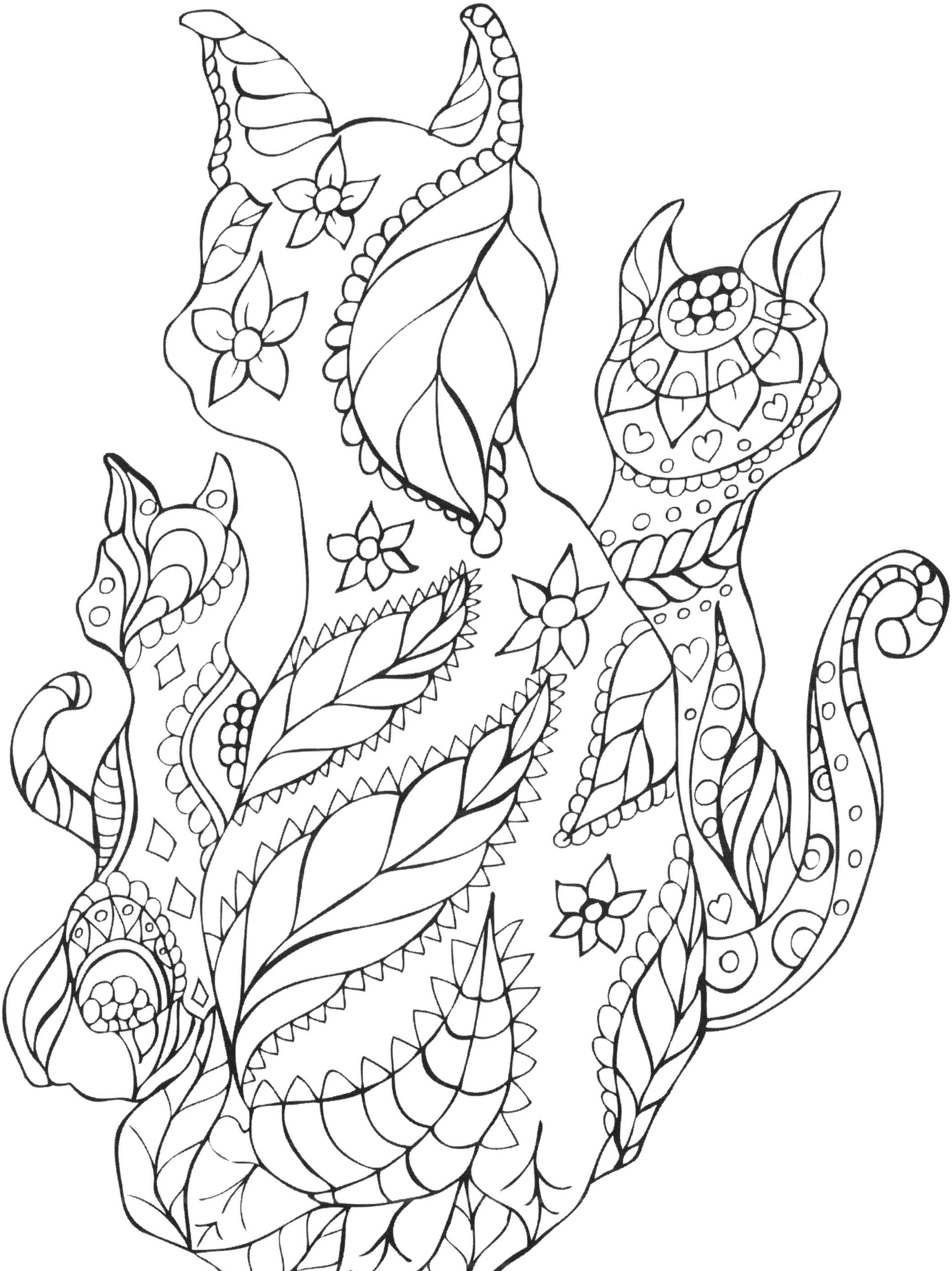

WWW.COLORINGCRAZE.COM

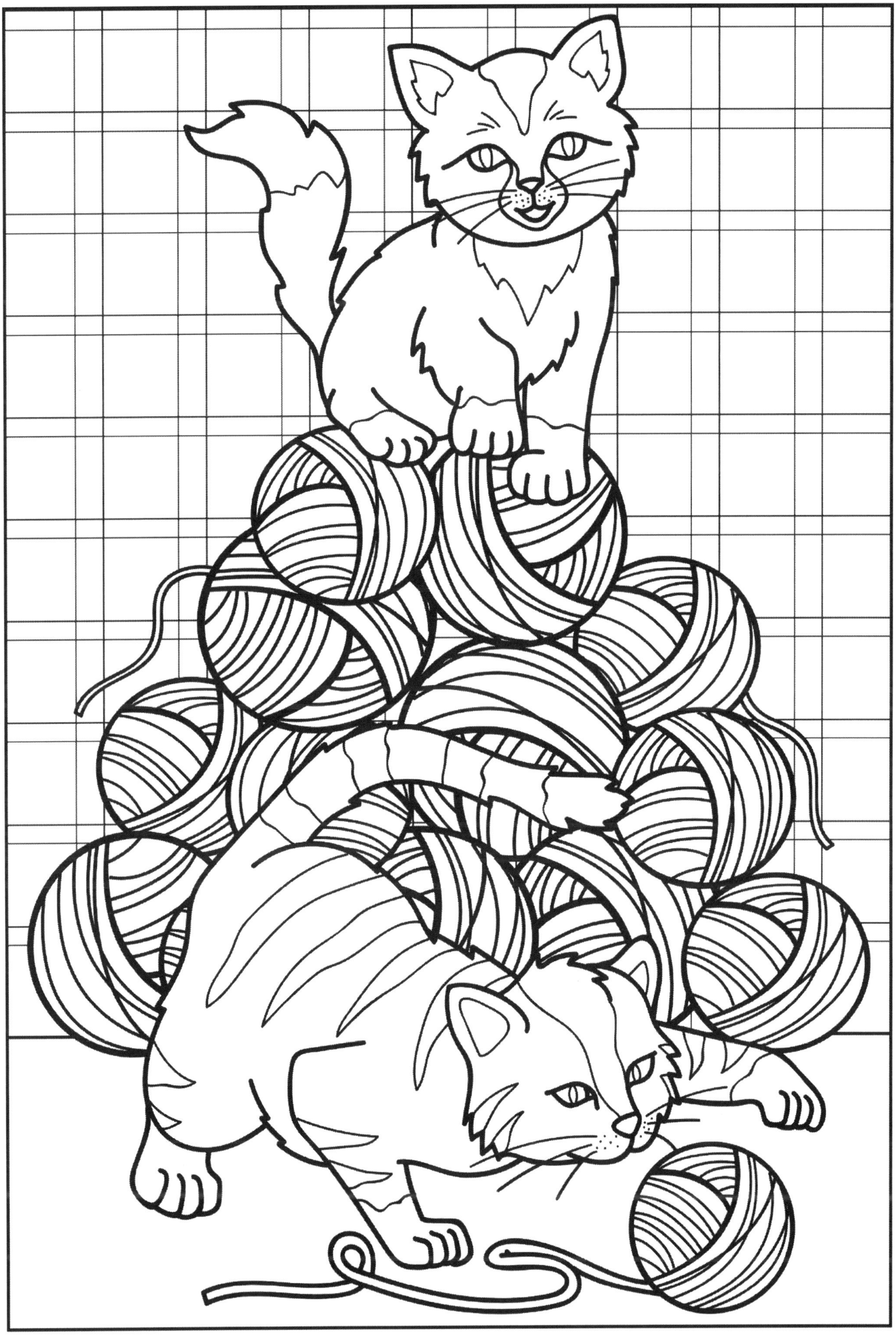

WWW.COLORINGCRAZE.COM

WWW.COLORINGCRAZE.COM

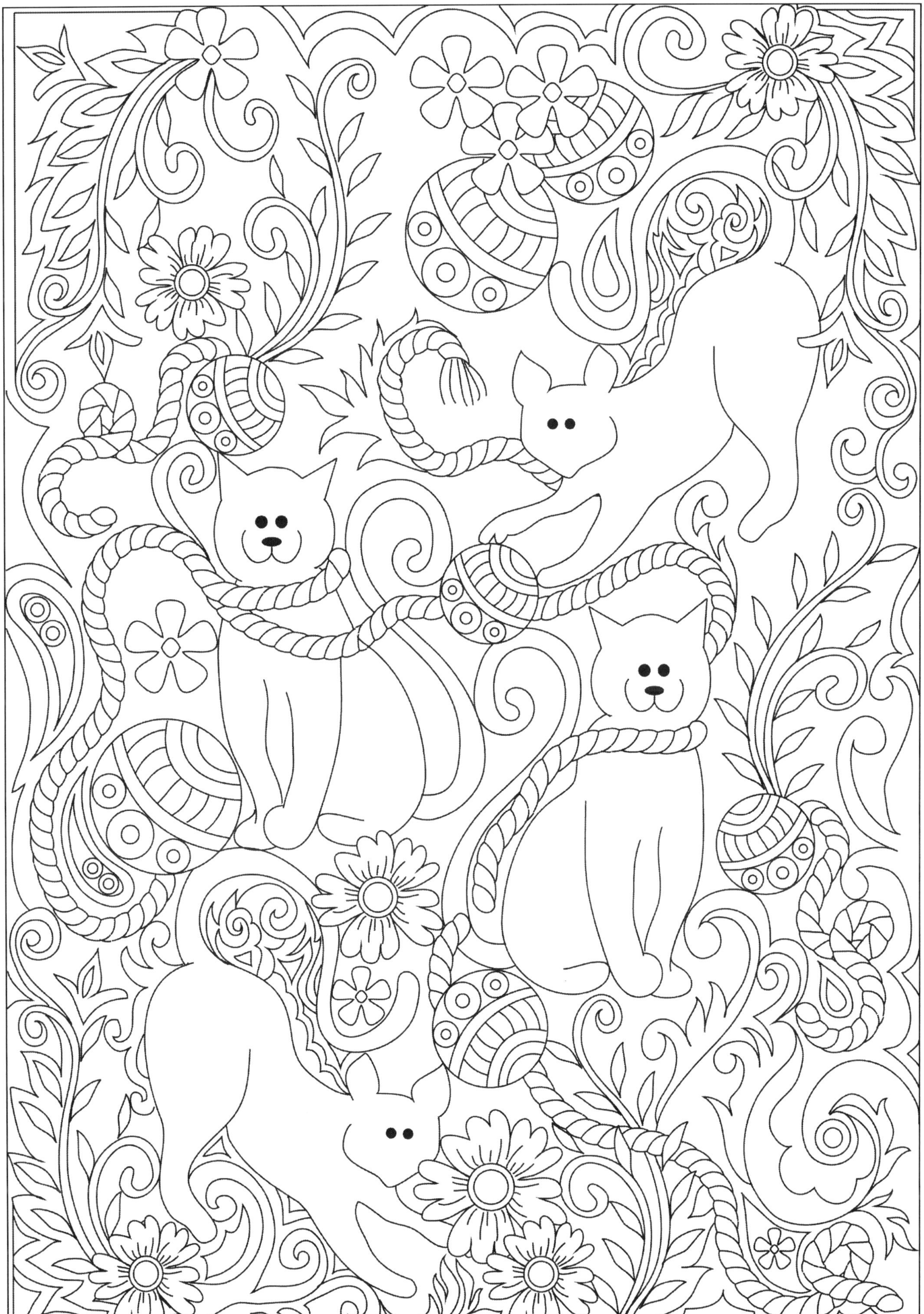

WWW.COLORINGCRAZE.COM

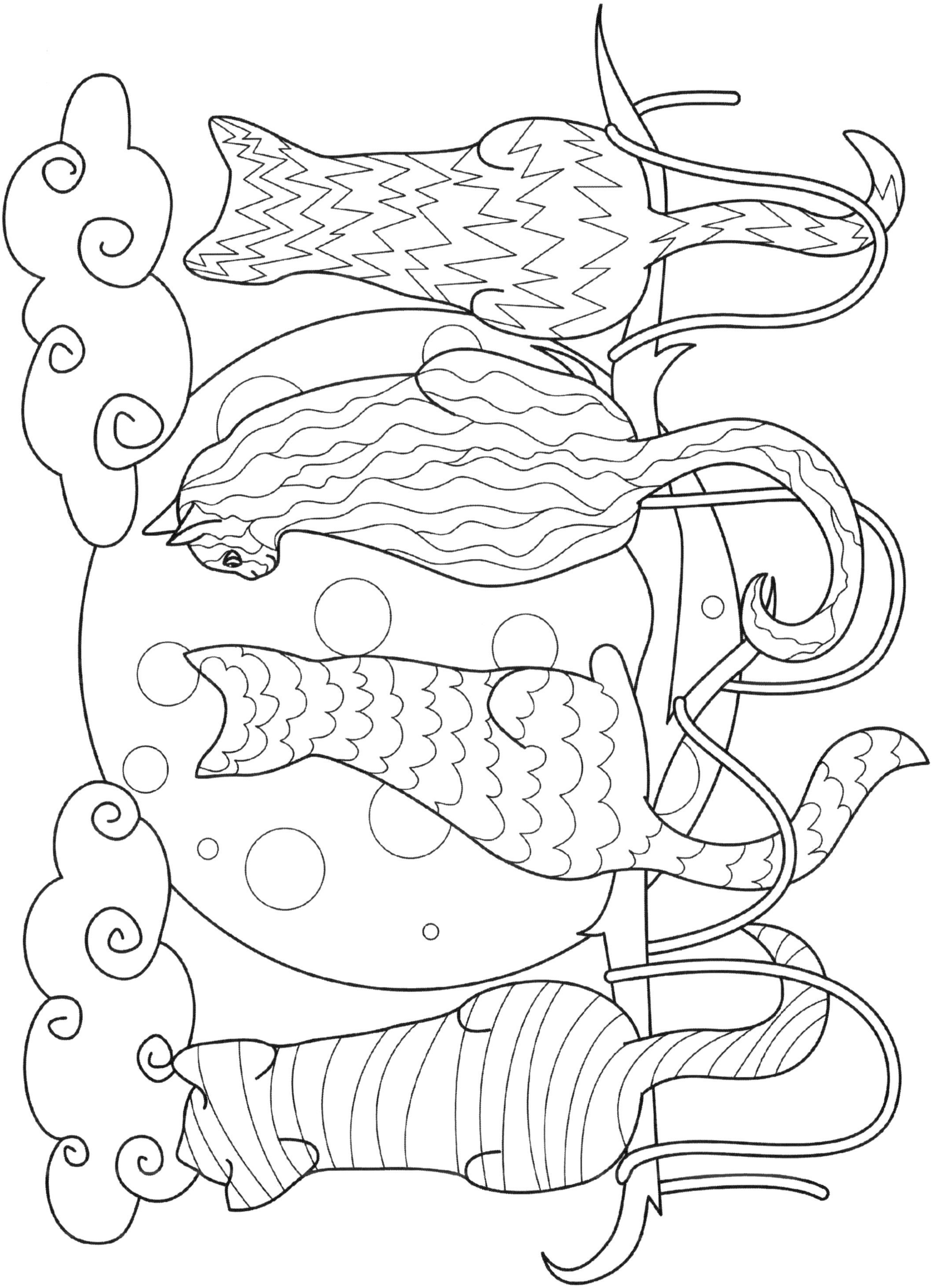

WWW.COLORINGCRAZE.COM

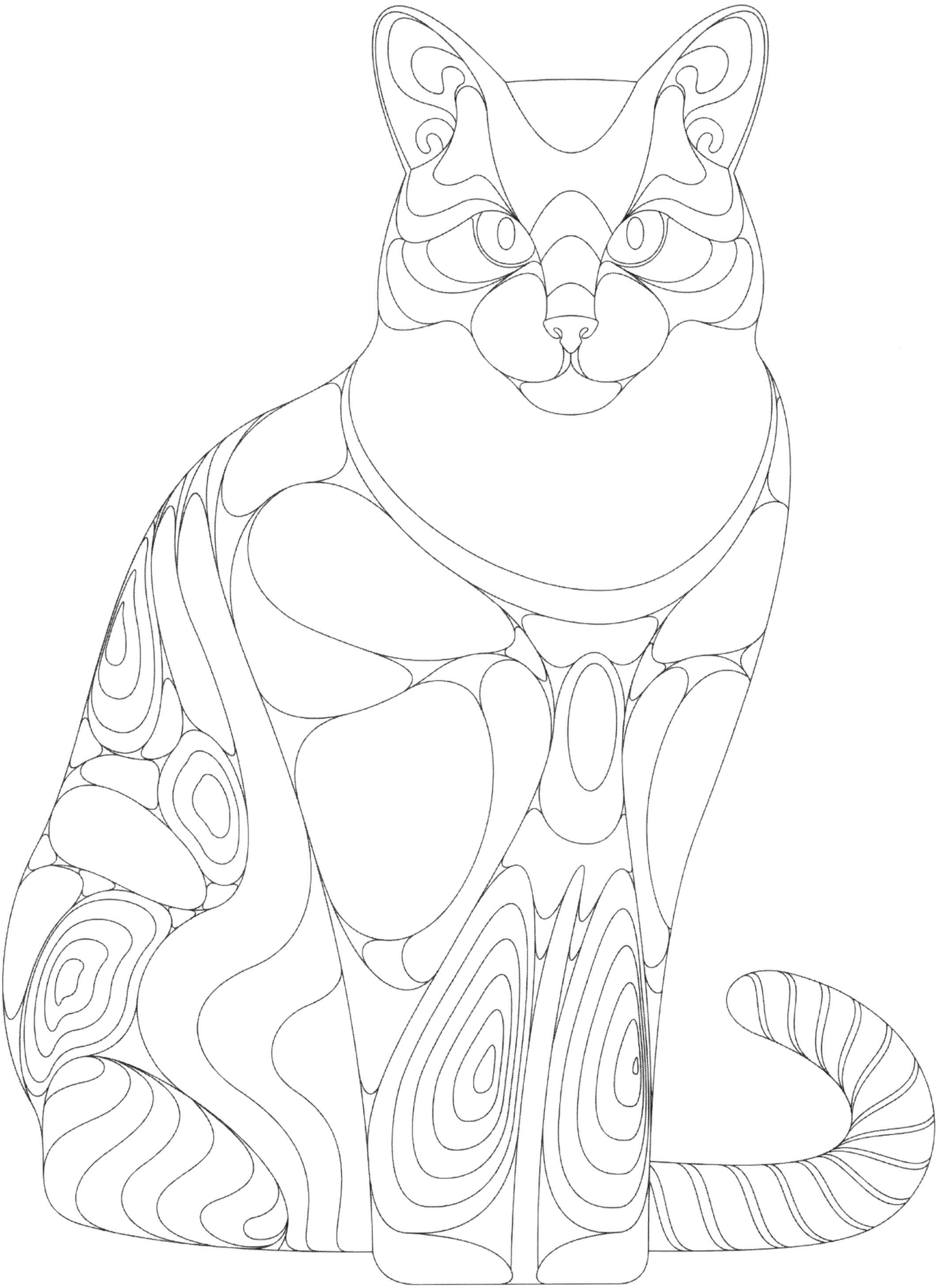

WWW.COLORINGCRAZE.COM

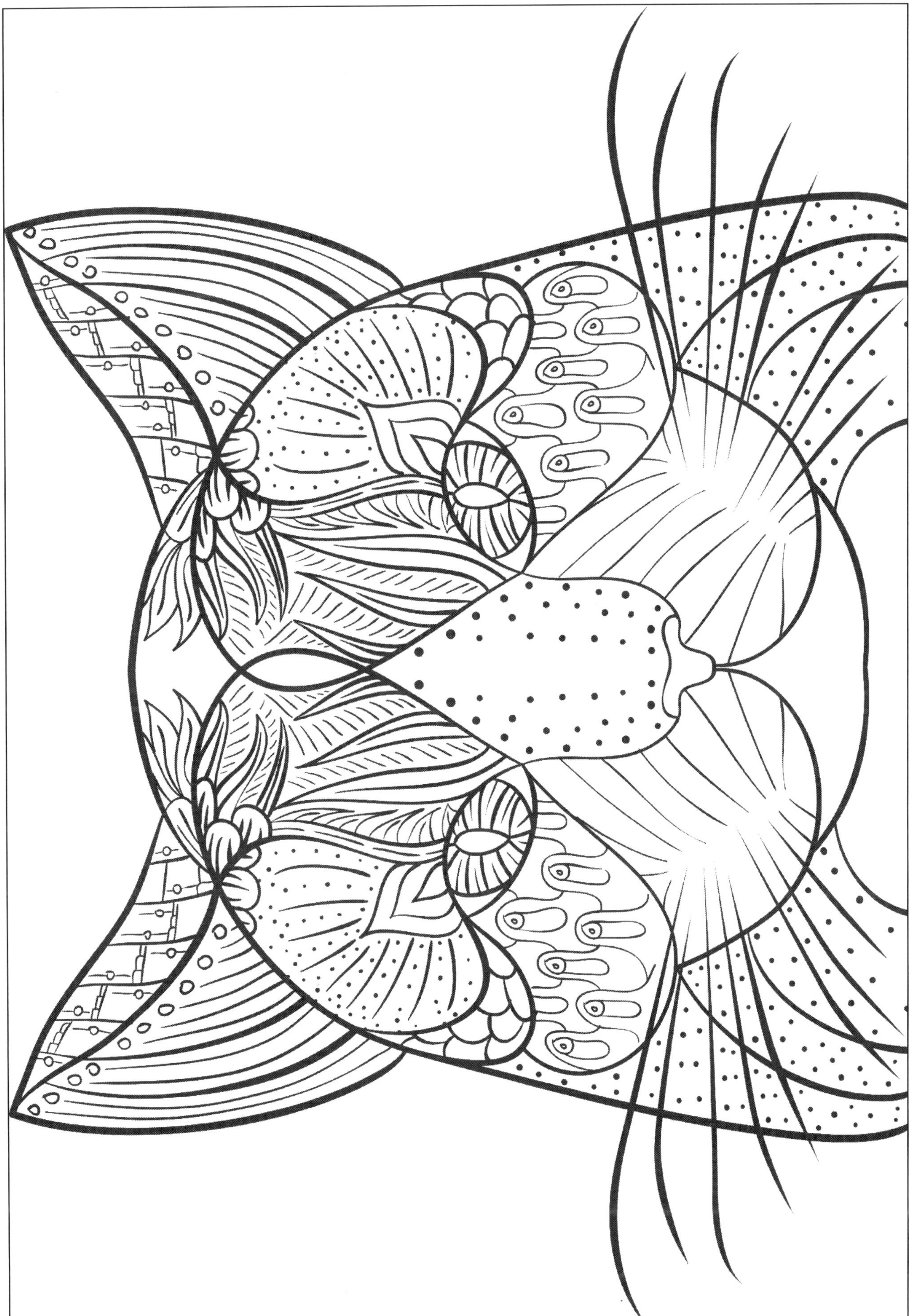

WWW.COLORINGCRAZE.COM

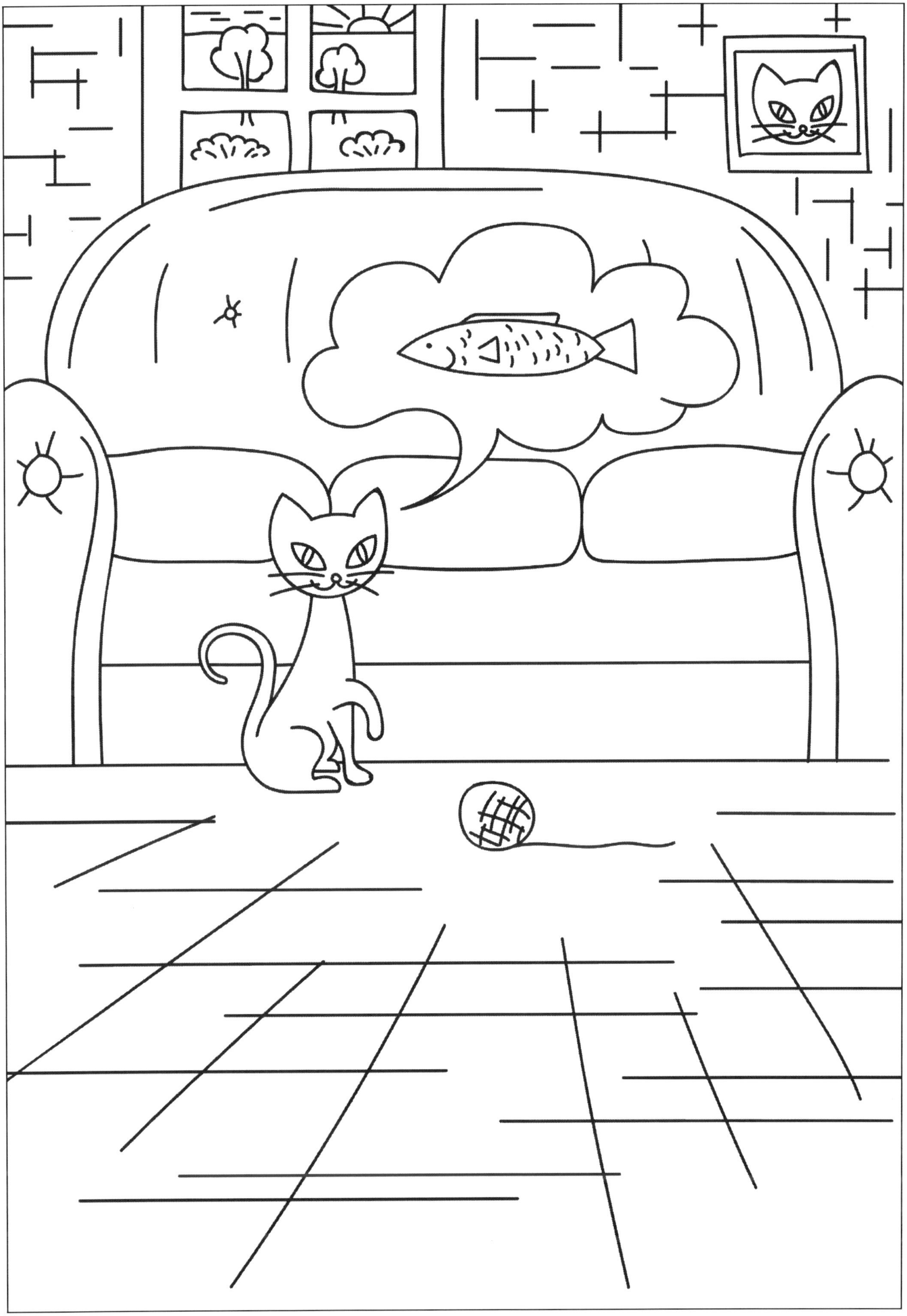

WWW.COLORINGCRAZE.COM

WWW.COLORINGCRAZE.COM

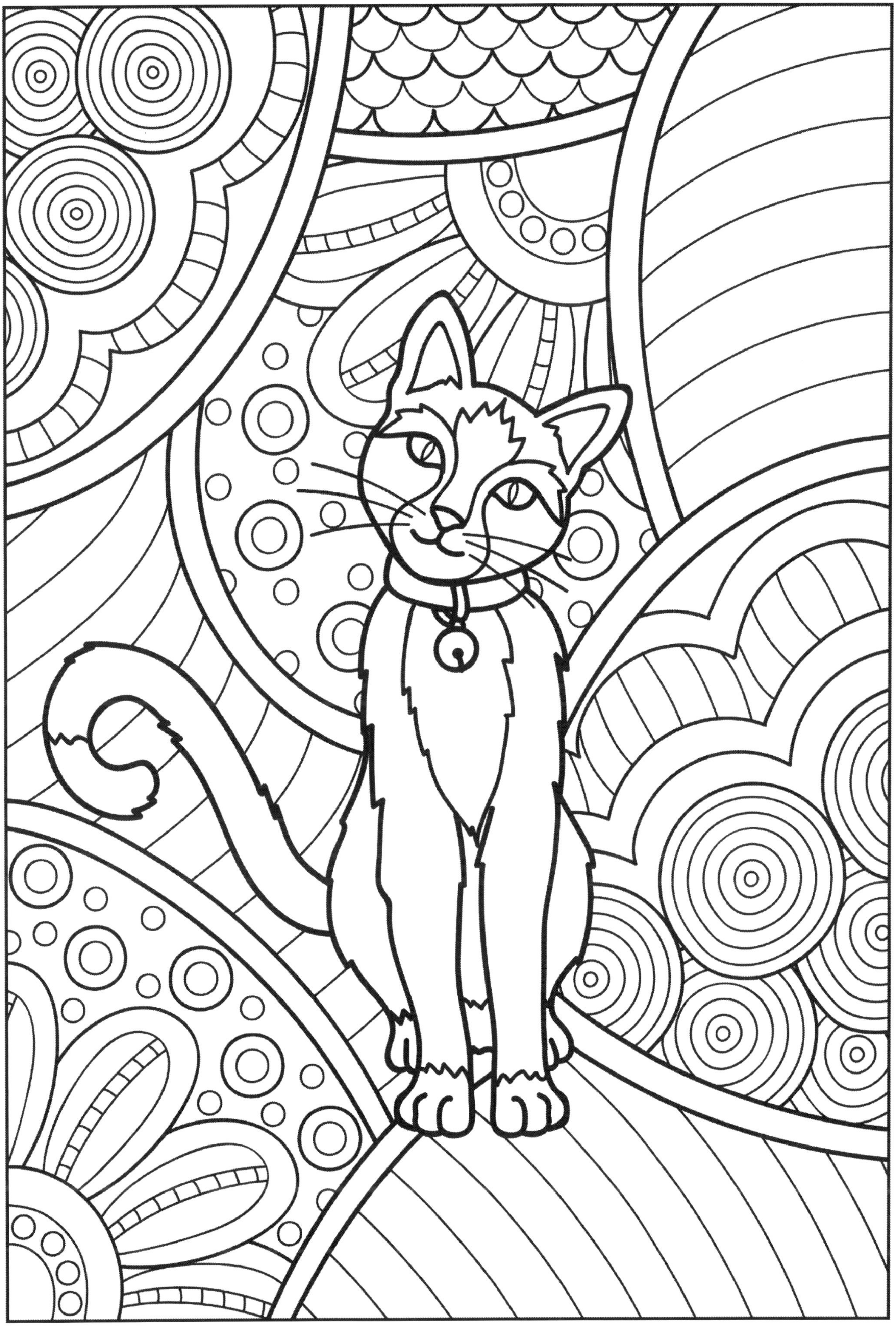

WWW.COLORINGCRAZE.COM

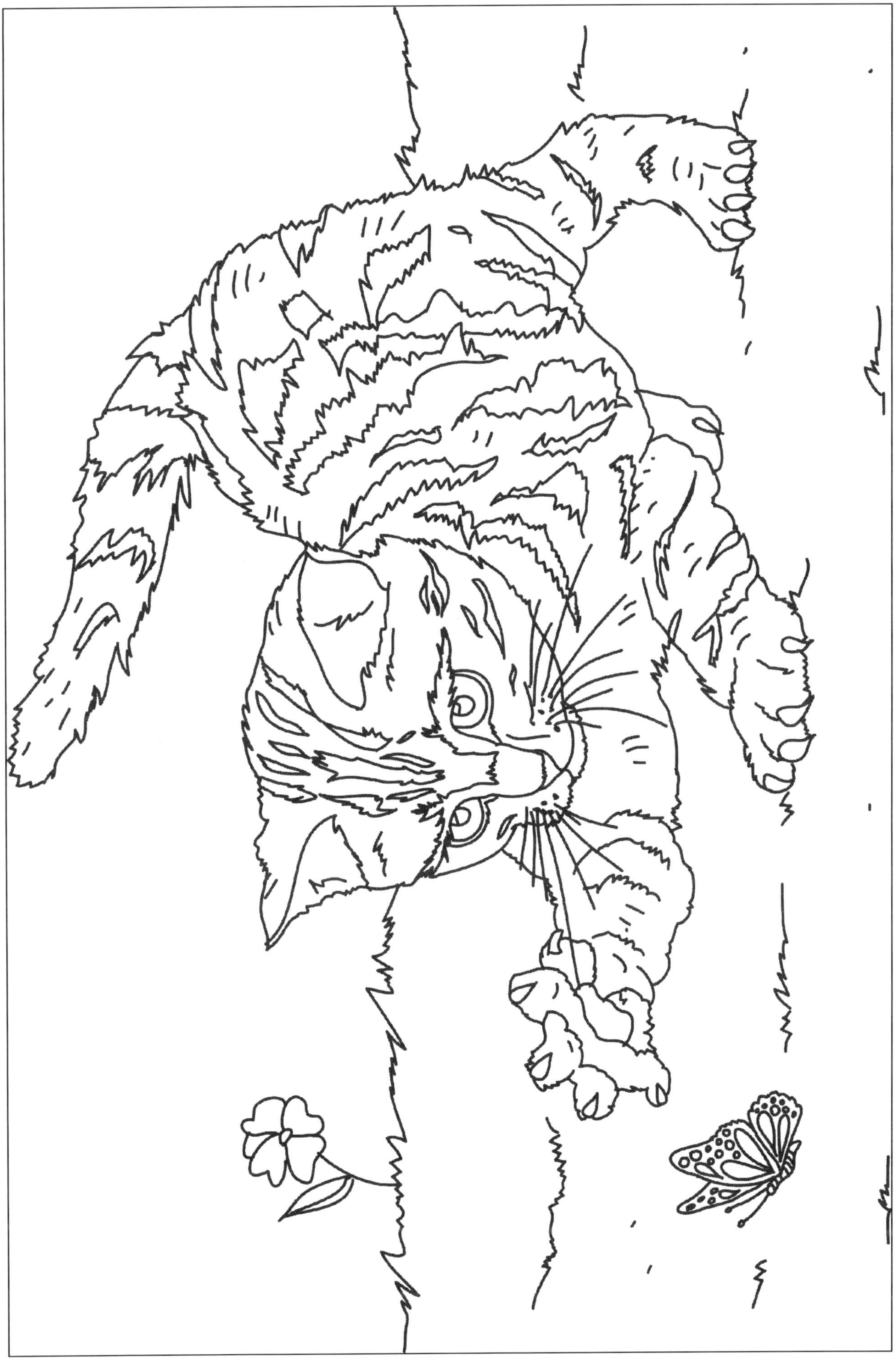

WWW.COLORINGCRAZE.COM

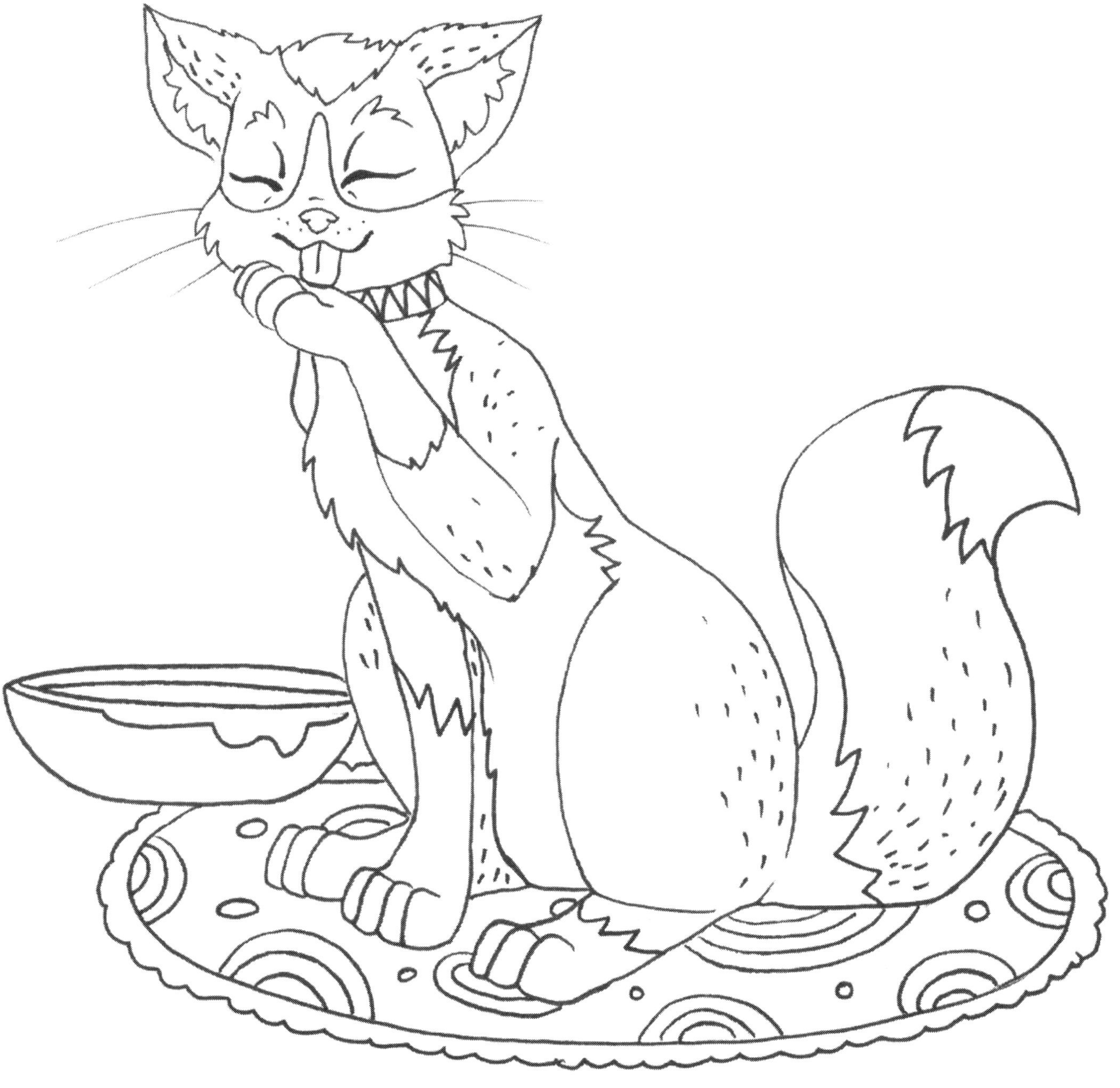

WWW.COLORINGCRAZE.COM

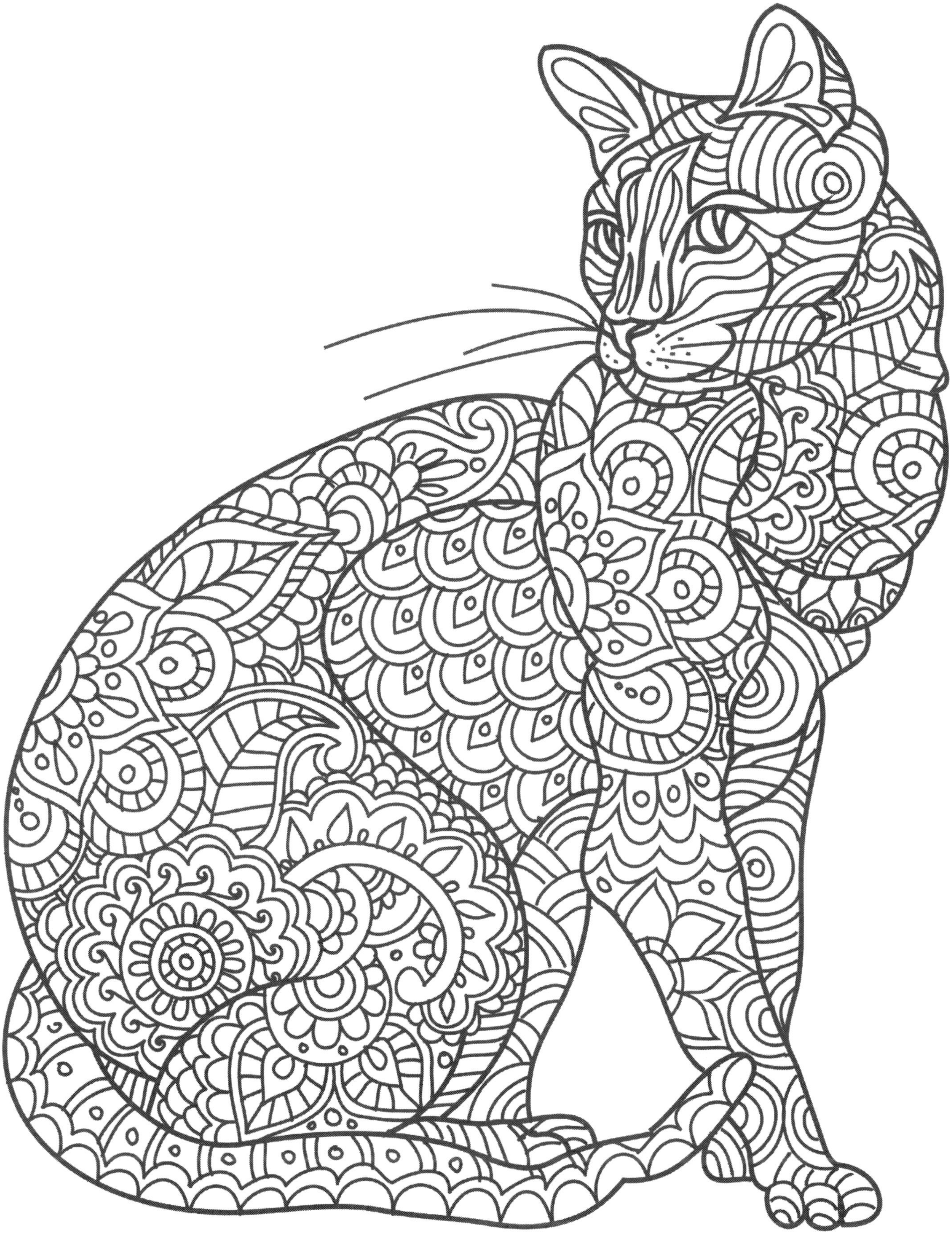

WWW.COLORINGCRAZE.COM

THANK YOU!

FROM THE AUTHOR

Thanks for coloring our book! I hope it was relaxing and I hope you had a lot of fun with it.

I would like to ask you for a *small* favor. Book reviews are very important for other coloring enthusiasts like you. If you have a minute, please leave a comment under our book here: www.coloringcraze.com/**review18**

It will help the buyers to make a decision and your feedback will be priceless to our illustrators ☺

All our other books are available here: www.coloringcraze.com/**our-books**

Remember to grab your **Free Bonus!**

=> http://www.coloringcraze.com/**bonus** <=

Thank You!

WWW.COLORINGCRAZE.COM

Printed in Great Britain
by Amazon